# PROMOTION POWER

*Five Disruptive Career Moves for Modern Women*

Dr. Lorri Goldmann

Dr. Neko Green

Dr. Dina Hernandez

Dr. Marilou Ryder

Dr. Tricia Thompson

PROMOTION POWER: Five Disruptive Career Moves for Modern Women

©2025 Dr. Lorri Goldmann; Dr. Neko Green; Dr. Dina Hernandez; Dr. Marilou Ryder; Dr. Tricia Thompson

All rights reserved: No part of this publication may be reproduced or transmitted in any form or by any means, mechanical or electronic, including photocopying and recording or by information storage and retrieval system without permission in writing from the author (except by a reviewer, who may quote brief passages).

ISBN: 979-8-9870551-9-9

Epub: 979-8-9927034-0-5

Library of Congress Control Number: 2025933549

The Publisher and the Authors have made every attempt to provide the reader with accurate, timely, and useful information. However, given the rapid changes taking place in today's job market, some of our information will inevitably change. The authors make no claims that using this information will guarantee the reader an employment contract. The author shall not be liable for any losses or damages incurred in the process of following the advice in this book. No warranty may be created or extended by sales or promotional materials. This work is sold with the understanding that the authors are not engaged in rendering legal, accounting, or professional services. Neither the Publisher nor the Author shall be liable for damages arising from the information within this book. The fact that an organization or website is referred to in this work as a citation and/or potential source of future information does not mean that the Author or Publisher endorses the information the organization or website may provide or recommendations it may make. Further, readers should be aware that internet websites listed in this work may have changed or disappeared since this work was written and when it was read.

Delmar Publishing

Huntington Beach, CA

Printed in the United States of America

Publicity Rights:

For information on publicity, author interviews, presentation, and subsidiary rights, contact:

Delmar Publishing drmlr@yahoo.com 760.900.0556

# CONTENTS

| | |
|---|---|
| *Introduction* | *v* |
| *The Back Story* | *vii* |
| *Why You Should Read This Book* | *x* |
| *Unlock Your Disruption Potential* | *xvi* |
| I    PUSHING BOUNDARIES<br>Challenging and Influencing Authority | 1 |
| II    ADAPTABLE AMBITION<br>Prepare but Also Learn to Improvise | 30 |
| III    SHINE BRIGHT<br>Find Effective Forms of Self-Promotion | 54 |
| IV    EMBRACE THE UNKNOWN<br>Welcome a Less Prescribed Career Path | 71 |
| V    RESPECT ABOVE ALL<br>Aim for Being Respected, Not Just Liked | 86 |
| *Lasting Impressions* | *103* |
| *Your Promotion Power Playbook* | *105* |
| *References* | *108* |
| *About the Authors* | *117* |

# CAREER TRUTHS

*Your work won't speak for itself- you must.*

## INTRODUCTION

Have you ever felt like you're hitting your head against an invisible barrier when trying to climb the professional ladder? Well, you are not alone. For years, women have been battling against the infamous glass ceiling, especially in industries where men have traditionally dominated.

I mean, seriously, think about it. Despite all the progress we've made, there's still plenty of challenges stacked against women when it comes to snagging those top leadership roles. So, there is some good news. After two decades of digging deep into the nitty-gritty of this issue, there's new research for women on the horizon, and it's eye-opening.

It turns out that it's not just external things holding women back; it's also our own inner demons. Yes, self-sabotage is a real thing, and it has been quietly sabotaging our career ambitions. Take job applications, for example. Women often hold back unless they meet every single requirement, while men are more like, *Close enough, let's go for it!*

And let us not forget the confidence factor. How many times have you held back from speaking up in a meeting because you were afraid of sounding dumb? I've heard that one too many times. But guess what? There's light at the end of the tunnel.

But self-sabotage and lack of confidence are not the whole story. Four doctoral students explored disruption theory, uncovering its game-changing impact. Inspired by the work of Whitney Johnson and Tara Mohr, they set out on a mission to find some unconventional strategies for women who are ready to shake things up.

We're talking about tossing out the rulebook of being the "good girl" and embracing a whole new mindset. And guess what? They recognized five transformative career skills that have been propelling women to the top. That includes things like rethinking self-promotion and challenging the status quo.

So, here's the deal: if you're tired of playing by the old rules and ready to make some serious waves in your career, this book is for you. We are laying out a roadmap for you to follow, one that's all about defying expectations and unleashing your full potential.

Seriously, it's time to ditch the self-doubt, embrace your power, and claim your spot at the table. Are you with us? Because this journey is designed to empower you to step into the leadership role you were destined for. Let's do this!

Dr. Marilou Ryder
Author and University Doctoral Professor

# The Back Story

In the world of academia, five curious minds came together: one faculty researcher and four driven doctoral students. Their quest led them to study a groundbreaking framework: five disruptive career skills first presented in a Harvard Business Review article by Johnson and Mohr (2013).

Fueled by the desire to empower female leaders, the four doctoral students set forth on a thematic study. Their mission —decipher the impact of these disruptive skills on women's ascent to executive leadership positions. But this was no solitary endeavor; it was a collaborative effort of research and ambition.

Under the mentorship of their faculty chair, they meticulously crafted research questions, survey instruments, and interview protocols. Together, they honed their tools, ensuring precision and reliability. And thus armed, they ventured into the realm of female leadership, seeking insights from diverse fields.

Meet the four peer researchers and their faculty advisor who spearheaded this inquiry:

Dr. Lorri Goldmann: Pioneering property management executives.

Dr. Neko Green: Guiding senior pastors to new heights.

Dr. Dina Hernandez: Championing Latina superintendents.

Dr. Tricia Thompson: Nurturing elementary superintendents on their journey.

Dr. Marilou Ryder: Advocating for women leaders.

In addition to the original research conducted for this book, Dr. Marilou Ryder incorporated findings from her prior research on women in leadership, drawing from her previous doctoral studies to deepen the analysis. This integration of past and present research provides a richer, more comprehensive perspective on the strategies and challenges women face in leadership roles.

Their collaborative efforts bore not just a study but a movement. A movement to equip all women with the skills they need to shatter glass ceilings, redefine success, and forge their path to upper management.

Join us as we delve into the untold stories of female disruptors, unraveling the threads of their triumphs and challenges.

## CAREER TRUTHS

---

*Strong women make waves. Make them anyway.*

# Why You Should Read This Book

**Show Me the Stats!***

Are you ready to uncover the stark realities of gender disparity in leadership? Brace yourself:

* Currently, only 10.4% of the Fortune 500 companies are led by women.
* Globally, women make up a mere 6% of all CEOs.
* Women CEOs often face longer paths to leadership compared to their male counterparts.
* Just 8.3% of chiefs of police are women.
* Despite strides, only 22.6% of general surgeons in the U.S. are women.
* Women represent 39% of all attorneys.
* Approximately 26% of school superintendents are women.
* In 2022, women surpassed men in educational attainment, with 39.1% holding degrees compared to 36.6% of men.

*As cited in various sources (see References).*

These statistics paint a vivid picture of the challenges women face in achieving parity in leadership roles across various sectors. It's time to dig deeper into why these numbers matter and what we can do to change them.

Ruth Bader Ginsburg (PBS News Hour 2015) once sparked a conversation about women's representation in leadership when asked when there would be enough women on the Supreme Court. Her response? *When there are nine*. This simple yet powerful statement has pushed society and organizations to rethink how they represent diverse groups, especially women. Like many other champions of equality, Ginsburg understood that having leaders who reflect the people they serve can truly transform organizations.

Research shows that women tend to shine in leadership, especially when it comes to inspiring others, offering support, and driving big ideas (Eagly et al., 2003). In fact, women frequently rank equally or even higher than men in skills associated with transformational leadership. Studies also indicate that organizations led by women tend to perform better financially, manage risks more effectively, and retain talent more successfully (Brahma et al., 2021). For example, female leaders have been shown to navigate crises more adeptly than their male counterparts (Zenger & Folkman, 2019). Evidence of this includes the fact that countries and states with female leaders experienced lower COVID-19 case rates and fatalities.

Despite evidence of women's leadership capabilities, there is still a disparity in senior leadership positions across industries. While women make up 58.4% of the workforce, they hold only 35% of senior leadership roles (Ariella, 2023). This gap becomes more concerning, considering that more women are earning bachelor's degrees than men, and they now represent an equal share of the college-educated workforce post-pandemic (Fry, 2022).

Specific industries like human resources, education, healthcare, and hospitality have higher rates of female leadership, but they also tend to have predominantly female workforces. For example, in education, where 73.6% of the workforce is female and only 18% of senior leadership are women (NSBA, 2020), having responsive, crisis-ready, and transformative leadership is crucial for success in K-12 education. With nearly three-quarters of the education workforce being female and roughly half of the student body also being female, it's essential to identify the factors that can help women break through the glass ceiling and ascend to positions of power within school districts.

If you're a woman looking to level up in your career, especially in a male-dominated field, this book is a must-read. Ask yourself:

* How can women ascend to senior roles despite these persistent challenges? Although women have made significant strides in education, the path to senior leadership remains an uphill battle.
* What are the key barriers hindering women's climb up the corporate ladder? Understanding these barriers is crucial. This book sheds light on the impediments and biases that may hinder women's professional advancement and offers insights into overcoming these challenges.
* How can disruptive career skills empower women to shatter the glass ceiling? Johnson and Mohr's framework of disruptive career skills offers a roadmap for breaking through the glass ceiling. By exploring how these skills

impact female advancement to executive leadership positions, this book equips women with actionable strategies for success.

* Why is promoting gender diversity in executive leadership crucial for organizational success? Promoting gender diversity is good for business. Research shows a strong correlation between gender diversity and financial performance. By amplifying women's voices in leadership, organizations can tap into new perspectives and drive industry growth.
* How can disruptive career skills reshape recruitment and promotion practices for gender equity? This book finds solutions. By identifying the impact of disruptive career skills on female advancement, organizations can reevaluate their recruitment and promotion practices, paving the way for more equitable gender opportunities.
* What lessons do successful women leaders offer to inspire the next generation of female executives? Sharing stories of women who have broken through barriers in their careers provides empowerment and inspiration to aspiring female leaders. It's a testament to what's possible when women leverage disruptive behaviors effectively.

*Promotion Power* champions women's advancement and equips them with tangible tools for success, going beyond just highlighting the struggles. Whether you are a seasoned executive or a rising star, the insights within these pages can help propel you toward your goals and pave the way for future generations of female leaders.

Now, let's dive into some groundbreaking career strategies tailored for today's modern woman, set within the framework of disrupting traditional career paths. Navigating the complexities of climbing the professional ladder can feel daunting and full of twists, turns, and unexpected challenges. But with the powerful insights from Promotion Power in your back pocket, you'll be ready to navigate the landscape and take your career to the next level.

Here is an exciting peek into five breakthrough career moves for today's ambitious women aiming to accelerate their careers.

## PUSHING BOUNDARIES: Challenge and Influence Authority

Forget playing the "good girl" role; it's time to shake things up. Instead of just nodding along with the status quo, channel your inner rebel. Stand out by questioning norms and proposing fresh solutions. Highlighting your critical thinking skills and ability to persuade can make you indispensable in any organization.

## ADAPTABLE AMBITION: Prepare but Also Learn to Improvise

Gone are the days of meticulously planned scripts. Embrace spontaneity and adaptability. While it is crucial to have a game plan, don't be afraid to think on your feet. Those off-the-cuff moments can often lead to ingenious solutions and unexpected victories.

## SHINE BRIGHT: Find Effective Forms of Self-Promotion

It is not about tooting your own horn; it's about showcasing your unique talents and contributions. Women excel academically, but it's time to translate that success into the workplace. Instead of shouting from the rooftops, focus on subtle yet impactful ways to highlight your achievements, like ensuring your team gets the credit they deserve.

## EMBRACE THE UNKNOWN: Welcome a Less-Prescribed Career Path

Ditch the conventional ladder-climbing mentality and embrace the scenic route. By being open to alternative paths and lateral moves, you will gain invaluable insights and experiences. Who needs a straight line to the top when you can forge your own trail?

## RESPECT ABOVE ALL: Aim for Being Respected, Not Just Liked

It is time to redefine success. Instead of striving for popularity, aim for respect. Be willing to make bold choices that command admiration, even if they are not the most comfortable or conventional. Shifting your focus from being liked to being respected can revolutionize your career trajectory.

We hope these disruptive career skills will empower you to break barriers and carve a path that's uniquely yours. So, grab your highlighter and some sticky notes, and let us embark on charting your path to success.

## Unlock Your Disruption Potential

Welcome to *Unlock Your Disruption Potential*. This quick self-assessment will help you evaluate your readiness for career advancement using proven disruption strategies. Reflecting on these questions will provide valuable insights into how well you're incorporating the five key disruption career skills into your professional growth.

*Directions:*

### 1. Read Each Question Carefully

Consider each question in the context of your recent work experiences and career aspirations. Think about specific examples and situations that reflect your current approach and behavior.

### 2. Choose the Response that Best Reflects Your Experience

For each question, select the response that most accurately represents how you handle the situation described. Use the scale provided to rate yourself.

### 3. Reflect on Your Answers

Once you have completed the quiz, review your responses to identify patterns or areas where you may want to focus on improving. Pay attention to questions where you rated yourself lower, as these could be areas for potential growth.

## 4. Apply Insights to Your Career Strategy

Use the insights gained from this quiz to inform you about your career development strategy. Consider how you can enhance your skills in preparation, adaptability, influence, and self-promotion to position yourself for career advancement.

## 5. Set Actionable Goals

Based on your reflections, set specific goals and actions to address any gaps or opportunities for improvement. Track your progress and revisit the quiz periodically to measure your growth and readiness for future challenges.

⁂

By taking this quiz, you are taking a proactive step toward unlocking your disruptive potential and confidently advancing your career. Good luck!

|   |   | 4 Definitely Yes | 3 Generally Yes | 2 Generally No | 1 Definitely No |
|---|---|---|---|---|---|
| 1 | I am eager to advance in my career and attain a higher-level leadership position. | | | | |
| 2 | When addressing disagreements with authority, I articulate my perspective clearly and constructively. | | | | |
| 3 | I maintain professionalism and respect in my interactions with authority figures, using data and facts to support my suggestions. | | | | |
| 4 | I build strong relationships with key decision-makers and am willing to take calculated risks to advocate for better outcomes. | | | | |
| 5 | I plan and prepare thoroughly for important meetings and am ready to adjust my approach when needed. | | | | |

|   |   | 4<br>Definitely<br>Yes | 3<br>Generally<br>Yes | 2<br>Generally<br>No | 1<br>Definitely<br>No |
|---|---|---|---|---|---|
| 6 | I balance detailed preparation with the ability to improvise, adapting my strategies and solutions as circumstances change. | | | | |
| 7 | While I believe in allowing my work to speak for itself, I have found ways to highlight my accomplishments effectively. | | | | |
| 8 | I have established a personal brand or narrative that effectively communicates my strengths and accomplishments. | | | | |
| 9 | I actively seek opportunities to showcase my key accomplishments and contributions, ensuring my network and colleagues recognize them. | | | | |
| 10 | I integrate discussions of my achievements into team settings, aligning them with my organization's overall goals. | | | | |

|   |   | 4 Definitely Yes | 3 Generally Yes | 2 Generally No | 1 Definitely No |
|---|---|---|---|---|---|
| 11 | I have taken a lateral move or a job outside my career field. | | | | |
| 12 | I have considered how a lateral move or job outside my career field could expand my skills and open new career opportunities. | | | | |
| 13 | In my career, I prioritize earning respect over gaining popularity, even if these actions are not well-received by everyone. | | | | |
| 14 | I regularly make decisions based on my principles and integrity, even if they might not be the most popular choices. | | | | |
| 15 | I have faced situations where standing up for my beliefs led to a loss of popularity but strengthened my professional credibility. | | | | |
|   | *Total Points in Category* | | | | |

Scoring: Total the number of points in each column.

## 55-60 ~ DISRUPTION DYNAMO!

You're a true expert in disruption strategies! Your savvy approach to career advancement shows you are ahead of the game and fully harnessing the power of these transformative skills. Keep leading the charge! Share this book with a friend!

## 45-54 ~ ON THE LAUNCH PAD!

You're well on your way to career greatness. You have a solid grasp of disruption strategies, but there are a few more areas to fine-tune. Focus on these, and you will be soaring to new heights in no time!

## 30-44 ~ TIME FOR A BOOST!

You're making strides but could use a career boost. Identify a few key areas for improvement and take action to enhance your leadership skills. You've got the potential; now, let's ignite it!

## 1-29 ~ WELCOME TO THE JOURNEY!

You're taking the first steps toward mastering disruption strategies. Reflect on these skills and consider partnering with a mentor to guide you through practical improvement strategies. Your journey to career advancement starts here!

# CAREER TALK

Tell Your Story—Or Someone Else Will. If you don't shape your own narrative, others will define it for you.

## Chapter 1

## PUSHING BOUNDARIES
### Challenging and Influencing Authority

*"I've always embraced a mindset of respectful questioning. When I challenge or push back, I focus on using my influence rather than confrontation to drive progress and rise to the top."*

Did you know that challenging authority can be a superpower for female leaders? In this chapter, we'll explore how boldly questioning the status quo can transform obstacles into opportunities, dismantling outdated barriers and ushering in fresh ideas that redefine leadership. When female leaders respectfully challenge authority, they inspire others to think differently and embrace new viewpoints. And guess what? This ability doesn't just stop at their desks; it can spark major positive changes and drive innovation throughout their organizations and industries. Most importantly, for women trying to get to their next leadership position, when executed effectively, challenging authority can lead to favorable recognition and pave the way for achieving the promotion you've long aspired for.

In both the workplace and personal environments, women find themselves navigating pressures to conform to authority figures' expectations, as highlighted by Johnson & Mohr's work on disruption (2013). However, breaking free from this mold is essential for professional career advancement.

Challenging authority is about having the courage to question outdated rules, propose smarter solutions, and push for progress. Imagine a female executive who refuses to accept an outdated policy that's holding her team back. Instead of staying silent, she speaks up, introduces a fresh approach, and sparks real change. When women take initiative and assert themselves, they don't just prove their leadership, they make a lasting impact (Novotney, 2023).

It turns out that women who've made it to the top of their careers aren't just good at following the rules; they're also incredibly skilled at challenging authority and driving innovative solutions within their organizations. While females are often commended in work settings for their compliance, W. Johnson and Mohr (2013) highlighted their adeptness at challenging and influencing authority. They illustrated instances where women refrain from merely echoing their superiors' sentiments, instead positioning themselves as indispensable within their organizations. Furthermore, they emphasized the skill of identifying problems and persuading others towards what they believe to be the optimal solution.

When women step up to challenge authority, they often bring in their knack for teamwork and a leadership style that focuses on inspiring change. By embracing these unique skills, they can create a more effective and inclusive leadership approach. Sometimes, women are hired during tough times to lead, a phenomenon known as the glass cliff, which shows how they break traditional leadership norms by taking charge in challenging situations. Women also tackle authority by balancing their family responsibilities with their work commitments. As more women take on leadership roles, organizations are likely to adapt to better support the needs of working parents, regardless of gender. Research indicates that when women have a say in senior leadership, it leads to more innovation and a more inclusive environment.

Sheryl Sandberg, Facebook's CEO and a leading voice in the tech industry has championed gender equality at work and challenged traditional norms and authority structures. Her book *Lean In: Women, Work, and the Will to Lead* has inspired women to pursue leadership roles. Sandberg's efforts have influenced corporate policies, promoted mentoring, and advocated for more women in leadership positions.

Politics is one field where the impact of women challenging authority is clear. Their influence has reshaped what was once a male-dominated arena, making strides in areas like equity and social justice. Women who challenge the status quo inspire others to follow suit, like Michelle Obama, who championed causes like childhood health and education.

But it's no secret that women who challenge authority face challenges. They might face backlash and criticism from those resistant to change, so it's essential to navigate these obstacles carefully. For example, in male-dominated workplaces, a woman challenging authority might be labeled as difficult or aggressive (Association for Psychological Science, n.d.). When women stand up to authority, some people might think they're not following the usual rules, which could make their peers and bosses think less of them.

# CAREER TALK

Stop Calling It Luck. You Earned It! Too many women downplay their promotions, chalking them up to luck instead of competence.

## VOICES OF POWER

### Women Who Challenge and Influence Authority

Challenging authority requires strategy, a bold push against ingrained biases and outdated norms to drive real change. In the world of leadership, where men have long dominated, women have had to navigate a labyrinth of expectations and stereotypes. However, within these corridors of power, the women interviewed in our study have not only survived but thrived, sharing their strategies and victories in challenging authority.

In every career, women face unique challenges when it comes to navigating authority. Whether it's breaking gender stereotypes, defending professional principles, or pushing for better organizational efficiency, the journey to success often involves challenging the status quo. Let's explore some essential themes that emerged from our interviews with successful women across various professions offering valuable insights and strategies for career advancement.

### Breaking the Mold

A lot of women find themselves pushing back against old-school gender expectations. There's constant pressure to fit a certain mold; be nurturing, but not too soft; be strong, but not too bold. It's like walking a tightrope, trying to balance between what society expects and who you really are. However, embracing authenticity and confidence can empower women to challenge authority effectively. Instead of succumbing to stereotypes, women can leverage their unique perspectives and skills to drive change in their organizations.

Consider a woman working in a traditionally male-dominated field like engineering. She might encounter stereotypes suggesting that she is not as technically proficient as the men or that she lacks leadership skills. In her workplace, she might face pressure to conform to these stereotypes by downplaying her expertise or avoiding taking on leadership roles.

To navigate these challenges and advance their careers, the women we interviewed embraced authenticity by confidently highlighting their skills and expertise. Instead of conforming to the stereotype of being less assertive, they asserted themselves in meetings, proposed innovative ideas, and sought out opportunities to lead projects. By breaking the mold and challenging these stereotypes, they not only prove their capabilities but also pave the way for other women in their profession.

**Culture Clash**

If you're a woman of color working in a space long dominated by men, you've probably felt the isolation and the unspoken pressure to fit in. For Latinas, African American women, and others in similar positions, the path to leadership can feel even more complicated. But here's the thing; many have found a way to rise by building strong alliances with other women. Instead of forcing themselves to conform, they've learned to navigate the challenges of gender and cultural bias with strategy, subtle influence, and the power of community.

One Latina vividly recalled, "I found myself in many meetings with all males, primarily white. I was the very first woman in over a hundred years, and I was definitely the first female Hispanic."

In these settings, being the only woman, or one of the few, means stepping into spaces where long-established norms are deeply ingrained. The challenge isn't just about proving competence; it's about balancing visibility and influence while navigating cultural and gender biases. Rather than conforming or staying silent, she takes a strategic approach. She builds alliances with other women, amplifies each other's voices, and finds ways to challenge the status quo without immediate backlash.

This account underscores the reality many female leaders face such as isolation, unspoken expectations, and the pressure to fit in. But it also highlights a key strategy, that of leveraging collective power. Women who forge connections, support one another, and approach leadership with both boldness and strategy can create lasting impact, even in spaces where they were never expected to lead.

**Stand Firm**

Have you ever felt the need to challenge the status quo but hesitated, wondering how it would be received? Standing up for your professional principles is a key part of leadership. Every industry has norms that sometimes need questioning and change often meets resistance.

Women in our study emphasized that driving progress means keeping the bigger picture in mind. Instead of simply calling out problems, they focused on clearly showing how their ideas could benefit the organization and everyone involved. By fostering open conversations and backing their points with solid reasoning, they found they could stand their ground while staying professional and true to their values.

For example, Maria had always believed that challenging the status quo was essential for progress. As a senior manager, she quickly noticed an outdated policy that required employees to work long hours without adequate compensation or recognition, a practice that was harming morale and stifling productivity.

Even though the company's leadership had long relied on traditional practices, Maria felt compelled to act. "I knew our team deserved better," she recalls. Rather than simply complaining about the issue, she began gathering data tracking overtime hours, employee satisfaction, and productivity metrics to build a compelling case for change.

Armed with concrete evidence, Maria scheduled a meeting with her superiors. In the boardroom, where most voices had long been dominated by veteran male executives, she calmly presented her findings. She explained how revising the policy to promote work-life balance would not only improve the well-being of employees but also enhance overall company performance.

Though her proposal met initial resistance, Maria remained resolute. She emphasized that her goal was to benefit the entire organization, not to simply challenge authority for its own sake. "Change isn't easy," she stated, "but sometimes we need to question old practices to create a better future for everyone."

Over time, her persistence paid off. The company gradually adopted more flexible work policies that recognized employees' efforts and rewarded efficiency, leading to a more engaged and productive workforce. Maria's willingness to stand by her principles, backed by data and clear, thoughtful arguments proved that one leader's conviction can spark meaningful change even in the most entrenched environments.

Opposing imposed or ineffective policies requires courage and conviction. Women in leadership positions often find themselves challenged by decisions made by higher authorities. Whether it's advocating for alternative solutions or highlighting the potential consequences of specific policies, women must be prepared to speak truth to power. By drawing on their expertise and insights, women can influence decision-makers and drive positive change within their organizations.

**Level the Playing Field**

Have you ever come across an unfair policy or practice and thought, *something must change?* The women in our study didn't just see inequality; they did something about it. They used their influence to level the playing field, whether by fighting for equal access to resources, amplifying voices that often go unheard, or pushing for policies that truly include everyone.

Real change does not happen by staying silent. These leaders believe that women must be bold in advocating for equity in their organizations. By speaking up, pushing for fairness, and making space for diverse perspectives, women are reshaping the workplace for everyone.

For example, Sophia, a respected executive, discovered a troubling trend while reviewing the company's internal reports. Despite performing the same work, women were earning less than their male colleagues, and employees from underrepresented backgrounds rarely found opportunities to advance.

Determined to address these inequities, Sophia embarked on a meticulous analysis of the company's policies. She scrutinized compensation structures, promotion criteria, and professional development programs, gathering clear data that revealed a systemic gender pay gap and limited career paths for minority staff.

Armed with her findings, Sophia called a meeting with the executive team. In a concise, data-driven presentation, she proposed concrete solutions: implementing transparent pay structures to ensure equal pay for equal work and establishing mentorship and leadership development programs tailored specifically for women and underrepresented employees.

Although some senior leaders were hesitant to disrupt long-standing practices, Sophia's unwavering commitment and the support of like-minded colleagues helped build momentum. She worked tirelessly to rally her peers, emphasizing that equitable practices not only fostered a fairer workplace but also drove the company's overall success.

Over time, the organization adopted Sophia's recommendations. The gender pay gap gradually narrowed, and more employees from diverse backgrounds began to ascend to leadership roles. Sophia's proactive approach not only transformed the company's culture but also set a powerful example for the industry at large.

By leveraging her position of influence and advocating for fairness and justice, this woman leader played a crucial role in leveling the playing field within her organization and creating a more equitable and inclusive workplace for all employees.

# CAREER TRUTHS

*Challenging authority is a leadership skill.*

**Courage Over Conformity**

Many women spoke about how important it is to stand up for what's right, fight for justice, and stay true to their values, no matter the situation. One woman recounted a specific instance where she challenged the board and her superintendent because they wanted to fire an assistant principal whom she felt was being treated unjustly. Similarly, she mentioned going to the school board to advocate for a change in policy, supported by data and personal stories. Additionally, she highlighted the priority of integrity over job security, expressing her willingness to lose her job rather than compromise her values.

For this woman, staying true to her values mattered more than just climbing the career ladder. She made it clear that every decision she made had to align with what she believed was right, even though it wasn't the easiest path. No matter what challenges came her way, integrity was her compass, guiding every career move she made.

For many women, prioritizing integrity and values over career considerations is an admirable goal, though it may not always feel attainable in every situation. Balancing ethical principles with career demands can be complex, as financial stability, workplace dynamics, and personal aspirations often come into play. While this woman's unwavering commitment to her values is inspiring, it serves as a reminder that integrity can be a powerful guiding force in one's career. When you let your personal values guide your work, you not only find deeper satisfaction, but you also build trust and show strong leadership, qualities that open doors to real career growth.

## Rewrite the Rule of Winning

Early in their careers, the women in our study didn't just accept the way things were, they challenged the status quo and reshaped it on their own terms. Whether it was challenging complacency or breaking through stereotypes, they reshaped what success could look like.

Take Anne's experience, for instance. "I refused to accept work that didn't bring me personal fulfillment and made a conscious decision not to settle for anything less than what truly mattered. That mindset gave me the courage to speak honestly and assertively when it counted, and it helped me navigate even the most challenging, male-dominated spaces with strategy and confidence."

And Alexa recounted how her suggestions were sometimes perceived as threatening by male supervisors. "I started reframing my feedback as questions," she explained. "It made me less intimidating and more approachable, which opened doors."

Another woman emphasized the power of taking thoughtful risks to advance her career. "Throughout my journey, I've leaned on respectful questioning and influencing skills rather than confrontation," she said. "This approach has helped me challenge norms, push boundaries, and steadily climb the ladder."

## Master the Mind and Message

How do women in leadership roles master assertive communication without conforming to stereotypes? The women in our study emphasized that speaking up had more to do with their confidence and finesse in speaking than it had to do with their actual volume. They became skilled in assertive communication, finding their voices without conforming to stereotypes. They knew how to grab attention in boardrooms while earning respect by knowing when to speak and when to listen.

For example, Grace faced challenges with confidence and assertiveness, defying stereotypes of women labeled as "aggressive" or "bossy." As one of the few women and people of color in the boardroom, she cultivated a leadership style that enabled her to advocate for herself effectively, earning respect and fostering collaboration without overshadowing the men in the room.

Emily highlighted the importance of being versatile and listening before speaking, which earned her credibility. Megan learned to wait until the men had finished debating, then spoke up with confidence, making sure her voice was heard and earning their respect along the way.

Communication goes beyond words; it's about understanding. These women mastered empathy, navigating tough situations gracefully. Their calm demeanor eased tensions, while their thoughtful approach earned respect. Their experiences show that effective communication involves not just speaking but also listening.

In our interviews, every female leader we spoke with highlighted the importance of recognizing emotions in challenging situations. They stressed the power of staying calm, finding common ground, and communicating in a way that keeps the conversation productive. Many shared simple but effective strategies, like pausing before responding to manage emotions and keeping their message clear and strong.

# CAREER TALK

Strong Opinions Don't Make You Difficult—They Make You a Leader. Stop softening your voice to keep the peace. Speak with conviction.

## Decide to Defy

Every decision is an opportunity to shake things up. Whether it was pushing back against racial bias or redefining what leadership looks like, these women didn't just make choices, they made bold statements. Barbara's strategic partnerships changed how others saw her, as she made tough decisions that underscored her belief that *respect cannot be compromised*. She also advocated for greater efficiency and smarter decision-making, which is crucial for moving forward. Effective communication and teamwork with stakeholders are key to successfully implementing these critical changes.

During her interview, Anna shared her experiences of pushing back against authority in boardrooms and council meetings, where she was often dismissed. She took the assertive approach of expressing her expertise without conforming to stereotypes, demonstrating great courage in standing up for herself. Additionally, she shared two instances when she had to make the difficult decision to terminate management contracts because of conflicts with clients regarding racial behavior, demonstrating a willingness to make tough decisions in the face of disrespectful behavior.

Anna shared, "In my mind, there are always multiple ways to approach a situation or a challenge. Putting things into perspective and leading by example influences others in the direction you are swaying them to go."

## Data-Driven Power Plays

Many women we spoke with relied on data to push for change. They knew that hard facts and numbers could make a powerful case and help turn ideas into action.

> *I think the data speaks for itself. You can't negate data. You can't argue data. In every aspect of my career, I've always used data as a driving force because data overcomes whatever biases and ideas you might have, and you can't argue with numbers.*

Tracy, a female director, illustrated how she used data as a catalyst for questioning disparities in educational outcomes:

> *When I got to that school, the majority of our students were not proficient and I questioned, well, what's going on? They had a lot of excuses. But I argued, 'What are the factors we can control?'*

By challenging excuses and focusing on controllable factors through data analysis, Tracy demonstrated a proactive approach to addressing educational disparities by leveraging statistical evidence.

The bottom line is that women who effectively used data to influence decision-makers and drive meaningful change within their organizations found that it enhanced their power and influence, propelling them towards leadership roles at the top.

## Navigating Stormy Seas

Women have a way of turning conflict into opportunity, even in a world where pushback is often misunderstood. Instead of shying away from challenges, they use them as moments to lead, innovate, and create real change. One leader, Alicia, refused to be labeled as "sharp-elbowed or pushy," while another woman leader shared how she set boundaries with clients, demanding mutual respect. Their stories remind us that negotiation is not just about compromise; it's about standing your ground.

Marcy shared an instance when clients disrespected her team, and she took a firm stand, insisting on mutual respect. This action exemplified conflict resolution and negotiation skills used with clients to establish clear expectations and boundaries.

She gave the following example: "I had these guys constantly coming into the office and complaining, and finally, one day, they came in, and I just said, *I want to help you, and I am not sure how to help you.*"

Another female leader shared her experience of being labeled as a bully because she pushed back and challenged authority. She expressed frustration, noting that men do not face the same scrutiny for similar behavior. She explained, "When I challenge and push back, I've learned to rely more on influencing skills than direct confrontation to move ahead quickly and advance in my career."

**Command the Room**

Navigating gender dynamics isn't easy, but the women in our study made sure their voices were heard. Despite facing dismissiveness and stereotypes, they spoke with authority, demanding respect. They balanced passion with professionalism while shattering expectations by speaking up, proving that a woman's voice is her greatest weapon.

The women reflected on the challenges and dynamics related to gender in the workplace, emphasizing the importance of doing the right thing, being heard, and gaining respect, especially in situations with gender disparity.

Bailey reflected on the need to balance passion with a calming voice, indicating an awareness of gender expectations in communication style. All the women leaders mentioned that being dismissed and having to navigate situations in which their authority is challenged was based on their gender dynamics.

Daria provided an example, sharing, "He always accused me of trying to stretch my authority and do things my way, regardless of what I said or did." She remembered being told, "This is my office, and you will do things my way."

Speaking up assertively and backing their statements with facts helped these women gain respect and advance to higher-level positions in their careers. Most of the women in the study highlighted the different standards women face, where passion must be tempered with a calm demeanor and factual support to be taken seriously. Even when they faced pushback or were dismissed, most of these women found that speaking with confidence was key. Standing their ground helped them break through gender biases, get noticed, and open doors to new opportunities.

**Cultivate Connections**

Behind every successful woman is a network of support. These women leveraged relationships and earned trust, paving the way for their success. They built on existing connections, earned the confidence of decision-makers, and used that trust to move their careers forward.

Sarah, an executive leader, expressed the importance of building connections and relationships in professional settings. She gave examples of how, over time, her boss has depended on her expertise, demonstrating trust. She recalled her boss saying, "I love that you always have an opinion and a voice, and I love that you have the company in mind."

She also said, "I have tried to continue with that behavior because people know what your impact is; they know what you are doing behind the scenes, which leads to trust."

Most women emphasized the power of strong relationships and persuasive communication in pushing for equity. Repeatedly, they shared how trust, rapport, and collaboration were essential to making real change happen.

Emily shared experiences about leveraging relationships to advocate for change, "Relationships are just an enormous piece if you're going to be a leader. I think relationships built upon trust ensure effective communication when bringing about change."

**Own Your Power**

Confidence is about knowing your worth and standing firm in your beliefs. These women faced challenges head-on, stayed true to themselves, and refused to be silenced. Their stories show that real confidence comes from conviction and the courage to lead with purpose.

All the women in our study discussed how having the confidence to speak up, share their thoughts, and stand firm on their principles led to career advancement. In reflecting on her career,

Mona shared her belief that anyone who desires to advance in their career must possess the confidence to speak up and let their leaders know about their abilities. She emphasized that sometimes, the quietest individuals on the team possess incredible talents but are often held back by fear or self-doubt.

For example, at a recent team meeting, Haley, a financial executive, encountered resistance to a new project proposal she had developed. Despite an initial pushback from some colleagues who questioned its feasibility, she remained steadfast in her belief in the project's potential. Drawing on her years of expertise and thorough research, she confidently articulated the benefits and addressed each concern raised with clarity and data-driven solutions.

Her calm demeanor and unwavering confidence in the project's merit gradually won over skeptical team members. By owning her worth and staying firm on her principles, Haley not only gained support for the project but also earned respect for her leadership and decision-making skills. This experience reinforced her belief that confidence is not just about speaking up loudly but also about believing in your ideas and effectively communicating their value to others.

## CAREER TRUTHS

*Speak up—even when your voice shakes.*

## PROMOTIONAL POWER MOVES

When women step up to challenge authority, they blend bold communication with smart strategy to spark real change. These *Promotional Power Moves* can help you make your voice heard, build strong connections, and create a workplace where everyone can thrive.

**Communicate with Confidence**

Speak up with confidence, no second-guessing, no holding back. Own your ideas and communicate with authority so people take notice. Instead of hesitating, trust what you bring to the table and say it like you mean it.

For example, in a team meeting, don't wait for the perfect moment; jump in, share your thoughts clearly, and back them up with confidence. Use strong, direct language that shows you know your stuff. When you speak like a leader, people listen.

**Prepare Strategically**

If you're going to challenge authority, make sure you're ready. The stronger your knowledge and expertise, the more weight your arguments will carry. Choose what matters most so you can grow professionally without burning yourself out. A mix of confidence, humility, and strategy will take you further than just knowing the facts.

Say you want to push for a policy change at work. Before speaking up, do your homework. Gather solid research, understand how your argument ties into the company's goals, and think about how to present it in a way that gets people on board. And don't forget the big picture; advancing your career is important, as is maintaining strong relationships and protecting your well-being.

**Seize Leadership Opportunities**

Step up and take the lead, whether it's launching a new project or improving something that's already in place. When you take the initiative, you're showing what you're capable of. It's a chance to make a real impact, build strong connections, and earn respect for your leadership.

For example, if your company's diversity and inclusion efforts need work, volunteer to lead a cross-departmental project to improve them. Taking the reins on something meaningful doesn't just shake up the status quo, it proves you're a leader who's ready to make things happen.

**Use Influence Tactics**

When pushing back against authority, facts are your best friend, but how you present them matters just as much. Confidence, charisma, and solid knowledge can help you make your case in a way that gets results. The key is to be clear, persuasive, and strategic in how you communicate your ideas.

Say you're pushing for flexible work arrangements to improve work-life balance; instead of just stating your opinion, back it up with data that shows the benefits for both employees and the company. Get others on board, build support, and present your case in a way that makes leadership see the value. Challenging authority is important, but influencing authority can open even more doors. Strengthening skills like negotiation, persuasion, and relationship-building can help you drive real change while also moving your career forward.

**Develop Emotional Intelligence**

Sharpening your emotional intelligence can make all the difference when it comes to handling tough conversations and making smart career moves. The ability to read the room, manage emotions, and build strong relationships is just as important as having the right ideas.

Let's say you're pushing back on a decision made by a senior executive. Instead of going in with just your argument, take a moment to understand their perspective. Acknowledge their concerns, find common ground, and approach the conversation with empathy. When you lead with emotional intelligence, you're more likely to turn a tough discussion into a productive one and maybe even gain an ally in the process.

**Defend Professional Practices**

Stand up for the professional practices that make a real difference in your organization or industry. Show why expertise matters in decision-making, and push for approaches that prioritize both effectiveness and fairness.

For example, if you see your company straying from the industry's best practices, don't stay silent. Speak up about why sticking to professional standards matters. Use real examples and solid evidence to make your case, ensuring that decisions support both organizational success and professional integrity.

**Advocate Against Inequities**

Speak up when you see unfairness in your workplace. Whether it's gender disparities, bias, or discrimination, your voice can help create a more inclusive and fairer environment for everyone.

If you notice certain groups are being passed over for promotions or opportunities, don't just let it slide. Start conversations, raise awareness, and advocate for fair, transparent processes. Use your platform to amplify the voices of those who are often overlooked and push for real changes that make diversity and inclusion more than just buzzwords.

**Foster Collaborative Relationships**

When it comes to influencing authority, relationships matter. Building trust and collaboration with decision-makers can give you the leverage you need to drive real change.

For example, if you're pushing back on a decision made by your department head, don't go in with just criticism; start with open communication. Show that you're willing to listen, seek feedback, and work together toward a solution that benefits everyone. When you build strong alliances, your influence grows, making it easier to create the change you want to see.

**Read the Room**

Know when and how to push back so it strengthens your position rather than creating unnecessary friction. Understanding the culture, power dynamics, and relationships at play can help you challenge authority in a way that's both effective and well-received. Before speaking up, take a step back and assess the situation and ask yourself, who's involved, how open they are to change, and what resistance you might face. Adjust your approach to make the biggest impact while minimizing unnecessary pushbacks.

By using smart, strategic moves, women can challenge authority in ways that drive real change and open doors for career growth. Confidence, emotional intelligence, and a well-thought-out strategy can help you break barriers and reach your goals.

## PARTING SHOTS

Challenging authority means more than just breaking rules; it's about rewriting them. The women we interviewed didn't just meet expectations; they exceeded them, showing the path for future leaders. They teach us that true power is about having influence, and that influence is earned, not given.

In short, challenging authority is crucial for women in all fields. By tackling gender stereotypes, standing up for professional values, fighting ineffective policies, addressing inequality, and advocating for better workplace practices, women can drive positive change and succeed in their careers. With confidence, bravery, and persistence, women can challenge authority and create a more fair and inclusive future.

So, are you ready to make your mark and take the next step in your career journey? Embrace the challenge, stand tall for what you believe in, and empower yourself to create a fairer, more inclusive future for all.

## THOUGHT-PROVOKING REFLECTIONS

### Reflecting on Personal Experiences

*Question*: Think about a time when you challenged an existing policy or practice in your workplace. What approach did you take, and what was the outcome? How did this experience shape your view on challenging authority?

### Applying Lessons to Current Situations

*Question:* Consider your current role and identify one outdated rule or practice that could benefit from being challenged. How would you go about advocating for change in this area? What strategies from the chapter can you apply to ensure a positive outcome?

### Preparing for Future Scenarios

*Question:* Imagine you are promoted to a leadership position where you need to lead your team through a notable change. What potential barriers might you face from existing authority figures, and how would you use your skills to influence and drive innovation despite these challenges?

# CAREER TALK

Hard work alone won't get you ahead. Visibility matters. Make sure the right people know what you bring to the table.

# Chapter II

## ADAPTABLE AMBITION
## Prepare but Also Learn to Improvise

*"Preparation is key. But just the nature of being a leader, you never know what day-to-day is going to be like."*

Do you ever find yourself navigating high-stakes situations at work, wishing you could respond with confidence and strategic finesse? Being able to think on your feet, especially under pressure is a game-changer for women wanting to get ahead in their careers. Johnson and Mohr (2013) found that men often thrive in these moments, using their strategic mindset and confidence to tackle challenges head-on, drawing from what they already know. This ability is a critical factor in their rapid career advancement.

Achieving success in leadership requires a blend of thorough preparation and adaptability. As women leaders, we must foresee challenges, make quick decisions, take calculated risks, and be ready to adjust our strategies as needed (Johnson & Mohr, 2013). This skill demands finding the right balance between being prepared and being able to adapt swiftly.

As girls and young women in school, we knew that being well-prepared was essential for success. However, in the workplace, the ability to improvise and adapt is just as vital. For women aspiring to leadership roles, it's crucial to harmonize these two aspects, to prepare thoroughly, and to have the flexibility to pivot when unexpected situations arise. This balance empowers female leaders to anticipate challenges and opportunities while navigating the dynamic nature of their roles. To thrive, women must develop the essential skills of quick thinking, decisive action, and calculated risk-taking (Johnson & Mohr, 2013). In a constantly changing world, those who can strike this balance effectively are not only better equipped to face challenges but also capable of inspiring meaningful change (Feld, 2021).

Oprah Winfrey's success story serves as an inspiring example, highlighting the importance of blending preparation with improvisation. Her journey is a mix of careful planning and clever adaptation (Garson, 2011). Oprah laid the groundwork for her future by earning a degree in communications and media from Tennessee State University. Starting as a local news anchor, she gained valuable practical experience. However, what set Oprah apart was her ability to seize unexpected opportunities. Faced with a setback in Nashville, she saw potential for growth and embraced a morning talk show in Baltimore, a pivotal moment of improvisation. This move propelled her to national fame. Oprah's authentic hosting style was another form of improvisation that deeply resonated with audiences, leading to increased ratings when her show was rebranded as "The Oprah Winfrey Show." Beyond television, she improvised by venturing into film, launching "O, The Oprah Magazine," and establishing her network, OWN. Oprah's ability to balance preparation and improvisation, shaped by her education, seizing opportunities, and developing her signature hosting style, has made her a relatable icon in media and entertainment.

Many female leaders, such as Jacinda Ardern, New Zealand's 40th Prime Minister; Mary Barra, CEO of General Motors; and Angela Merkel, former Chancellor of Germany, are known for their ability to seamlessly combine preparation with improvisation (Cursa). Ardern, for example, is renowned for her meticulous planning and evidence-based policies, paired with remarkable adaptability during crises such as the COVID-19 pandemic. Barra combines deep technical expertise with a forward-thinking approach to innovation, while Merkel's commitment to thorough research consistently guided her decisive actions in navigating complex challenges.

However, this approach is not without its challenges. Gender stereotypes often result in women's improvisational skills and preparedness being undervalued or overlooked, which can limit opportunities for growth and advancement. This lack of recognition and support can be disheartening, leading some women to hesitate to embrace new challenges. Additionally, many women grapple with Imposter Syndrome, fostering self-doubt and reluctance to take risks.

In the next section, Voices of Power, we'll delve into the experiences of women leaders who have successfully navigated these obstacles. They share their stories and strategies for balancing preparation with improvisation, offering inspiration and practical insights for overcoming these barriers.

# CAREER TRUTHS

*You don't have to be in charge to take charge.*

## VOICES OF POWER

## Women Who Blend Preparation with Improvisation

Benjamin Franklin famously said, "By failing to prepare, you are preparing to fail" (Mayberry, 2016). However, while preparation sets the stage, it may not foresee unexpected challenges or crises that demand immediate responses.

According to Johnson and Mohr (2013), improvisation is not about being unprepared but about trusting one's knowledge and instincts. This skill is essential for organizational agility, allowing leaders to adapt quickly in dynamic environments (Mannucci et al., 2021). Women who embrace improvisation excel at managing unforeseen obstacles, navigating regulatory changes, and meeting the ever-evolving demands of leadership.

## Talk Smarter, Lead Stronger

Effective communication emerged as a consistent theme for all the women in our studies. Jazmyne, an executive, encountered a challenging situation during a high-stakes client meeting. She had prepared extensively for the presentation but unexpectedly faced resistance from a senior stakeholder who questioned key aspects of the proposal. Instead of becoming defensive, Jazmyne remained composed and recalibrated her approach on the spot.

She calmly acknowledged the concerns raised, adjusting her tone to convey confidence and openness to alternative viewpoints. By managing her perception through measured responses and maintaining a professional demeanor, Jazmyne effectively improvised to address unexpected objections. She used nonverbal cues such as maintaining eye contact and attentive body language to convey reassurance and credibility.

In doing so, Jazmyne not only salvaged the meeting but also demonstrated her ability to adapt and communicate effectively under pressure. This example highlights how effective communication, both verbal and nonverbal, can play a pivotal role in navigating challenges and achieving successful outcomes in professional settings.

Women leaders also mentioned the importance of managing their perception, tone, and passion to avoid being seen as not prepared, which is also a focus on effective communication because they had to improvise to get their point across. In situations where you're caught off guard, the key is to remain composed. Maintain calm, project confidence, and stay in control.

## The Curveball

Women leaders who excel at blending preparation with improvisation emphasize adaptability in how they lead. They know that leadership can throw curveballs, so while being prepared is crucial, they're also ready to tackle whatever comes their way each day.

In our study, many women leaders stressed the importance of adjusting their leadership styles to fit different situations. Sonia, a high-level director, put it perfectly: "Preparation is key... but as a leader, you never really know what each day will bring."

Another leader highlighted the power of teamwork in problem-solving, saying, "I'm all about figuring things out together. Let's partner up to solve these challenges."

And then there's the aspect of continuous learning. One woman summed it up nicely: "Being a leader means always being open to learning and adapting." These insights show that leadership is all about ongoing learning, teamwork, and being ready for whatever surprises come your way. Being adaptable in your leadership approach can be invaluable when confronted with unforeseen challenges. For instance, if a key team member unexpectedly resigns, quickly reassessing team dynamics and swiftly delegating responsibilities can help maintain productivity and morale during the transition.

**On the Fly**

During the COVID-19 Pandemic, these leaders faced a lot of uncertainty. They had to make critical decisions on the fly without much time for planning. It really showed how agility and quick thinking are crucial in a crisis.

Talking to these female leaders, you could see how much uncertainty they had to navigate. One woman described it as "the most uncertain period" of her career saying, "I had everything planned out, and then COVID hit, I had to improvise like never before."

It's clear that in times of crisis, being able to adapt and make decisions quickly can make all the difference. Many of the school superintendents noted that they prepare in their heads 100% of the time, whether in the office or out doing things in the community. They are constantly thinking, "What happens next? How do I prepare for later? What's going on in the long term?" Several noted that the more someone plans, the less they must do it.

All our women leaders stressed how important it is to be ready for unexpected events. One woman compared being prepared to how teachers plan lessons: "You can have a solid plan, but you've got to think ahead about what could go wrong and get more info." Another agreed, saying superintendents have a significant role in crises: "When things get tough, people need to see you jumping in and helping fix things." And another added, "Sometimes you've just got to act fast and change things up."

## When Things Get Tough, Listen

The women participants in our study showed how balancing preparation with flexibility helps them make a real difference for the people they serve. Many highlighted the importance of reading the room in stressful situations or when making critical decisions. While they initially had their own ideas about what would benefit their organizations most, they recognized the importance of humility in listening to and understanding all stakeholders. This flexible and reflective leadership approach resulted in significant positive impacts.

For example, during a major restructuring initiative, Frieda, an aspiring CEO, initially planned a specific course of action to streamline operations. However, after consulting with frontline staff and considering their input, she adjusted her strategy to accommodate their needs and concerns better. This collaborative approach not only improved employee morale but also led to more effective implementation of the restructuring plan, benefiting the entire organization.

## CAREER TRUTHS

---

*Being 'likable' is overrated—being respected is non-negotiable.*

## The Humble Leader

We have all learned that being open and humble is crucial for good leadership. These women shared how important it is to be willing to listen to others and consider different ideas that can shape your career. Marci, who worked as an assistant superintendent, talked about times when she trusted her boss's decisions even though she had her own ideas. It showed how open she was to different viewpoints and how that helped her grow in her career.

She also pointed out how being defensive or stubborn can hold you back. People notice when leaders are open to different opinions and make wise choices based on valuable information.

Alicia said, "So I think leaders appreciate that I am honest enough to give them open feedback and tell them what will happen and why. I think it is important that you really see things through other people's eyes."

Preparing and improvising have a lot to do with whether an individual is humble and open-minded to solutions beyond their own. One woman talked about her position as an assistant superintendent and how she had to step back many times to respect the superintendent's decision.

This level of humility, even with her extensive decision-making experience, demonstrated her ability to stay open-minded. She shared how being seen supporting her leader, rather than resisting, had a surprisingly positive effect on her career. She also reflected on the importance of handling disagreements thoughtfully, acknowledging that while it's easy to get defensive or insist on being right, people ultimately pay attention to how you navigate those moments and the path you decide to take.

## A Delicate Balance

A female minister shared how she understood the delicate balance of authority and flexibility in dynamic ministry environments. For her, being ready for anything while also being able to adapt was key. She shared a personal example from a new church role where she had to step up quickly when the worship pastor left unexpectedly:

> *When I joined the team, the worship pastor had just left without a replacement. They asked me to step in right away. It was a rapid shift from zero to a hundred. The team environment was toxic and unhealthy, and I wasn't even sure if everyone knew Jesus. I had to balance authority while also addressing these deeper issues. It was a shift from focusing solely on the Sunday service to tackling fundamental issues within the church leadership.*

Everyone in our study agreed that being able to adapt to challenges played a huge role in moving up within their organizations. Those who could pivot when needed while staying clear on their priorities were seen as strong leadership candidates. Hiring committees valued people who were both reflective and forward-thinking, leaders who could handle tough situations while staying steady and focused.

## The Power of Perception

While being prepared is crucial, these female leaders also value being completely focused and responsive at the moment. They adjust their approach as things change, making sure they stay effective and engaged in every situation.

Even though many of their stories involved significant challenges, staying present and attentive in smaller moments was a common thread. Nan stressed the balance between preparing and being present in meetings and presentations, saying, "I try not to over-prepare so I can stay fully in the moment. Things change, and we need to adapt our responses accordingly."

Breta talked about how personal connection matters in stakeholder meetings, pointing out the importance of listening actively and reflecting on what's said. She highlighted that impressions aren't just formed through emails but also through informal chats and meetings, showing how genuine engagement shapes leadership interactions.

Although many experiences shared by these women were large-scale in nature, the topic of being present came up frequently. One of the seemingly little moments discussed in preparing but also learning to improvise was the idea of being present and reading the room during presentations or meetings. Tamara noted that she would "try hard not to be so prepared that you can't listen and be present at the moment because these moments change, and your reaction to them must change as well."

## PROMOTIONAL POWER MOVES

It's not easy to lead on the fly. We all love a plan, but we have also learned that if a woman wants to get ahead in her career, it is crucial to know how to blend preparation with improvisation. If you desire to move ahead in your leadership career, here are some actionable strategies that you can begin to work on now.

# CAREER TALK

Confidence Comes From Doing, Not Just Preparing. You can't wait until you "feel ready" to step up. Take the shot, adjust as you go.

## Stay Ahead of the Curve

Stay ahead by keeping up with industry trends, leadership strategies, and new technologies. The more you know, the more adaptable and innovative you can be when change inevitably happens.

Take, for example, a woman leader in tech who makes learning a priority. She attends conferences, stays on top of the latest research, and builds a strong network. When a new technology shakes up the industry, she doesn't panic, she jumps into online courses and workshops to get ahead of the curve.

By staying curious and proactive you're putting yourself in a position to lead, solve problems, and drive real innovation in your organization.

## Get Into Their Shoes

Emotional intelligence, as we mentioned in the previous section, is a game-changer for any leader. As a woman leader, strengthening your emotional intelligence starts with self-awareness, empathy, and building real connections.

Start by checking in with yourself regularly-reflect on your emotions, strengths, and areas for growth. Pay attention to how your feelings shape your decisions and interactions. The more you understand yourself, the better you'll be at leading others.

Empathy is just as important. Really listen to your team, what they're saying, what they're not saying, and what might be driving their concerns. Put yourself in their shoes and consider how their experiences shape their perspectives.

And don't just work with people, get to know them. Build trust, foster teamwork, and create an environment where open communication is the norm. Strong relationships make it easier to tackle challenges, resolve conflicts, and keep your team motivated and engaged. When respect goes both ways, you're not just leading, you're inspiring.

### Fuel Your Future: Find a Mentor

Women learn early in their careers that having a mentor is essential. If you've got one (and if you're reading this book, you should by now), make the most of that relationship. Talk to them about how to balance being prepared with staying flexible. And don't stop there; ask for feedback from colleagues and higher-ups to catch any blind spots that could sharpen your decision-making skills.

Look for mentors who've been through the ups and downs of leadership and know how to handle unpredictable situations. They can offer real-world advice on crisis management, quick thinking, and staying steady under pressure, things you don't always learn in a textbook. Sometimes, their feedback will point out things you never even considered, giving you a fresh perspective on how to adapt and lead with confidence.

Keep those conversations going. Ask your mentor how they've handled tricky situations, what worked, and what didn't. The more you learn from their experiences, the stronger your leadership toolkit becomes. Seeking out mentorship and feedback is all about continuously growing, staying sharp, and leading with confidence, no matter what comes your way.

## CAREER TRUTHS

*Be bold enough to say, "This isn't working.*

## Build a Culture of Bold Ideas

As a woman leader on the rise, one of the most powerful things you can do is create a space where your team feels comfortable sharing ideas. When people feel heard and supported, they're more likely to think outside the box and bring fresh solutions to the table.

Start by making sure your team knows their input matters. During meetings and brainstorming sessions, actively invite ideas without shutting people down or letting the same voices dominate the conversation. If your team trusts that their ideas will be taken seriously, they'll be more willing to speak up.

You can also set up simple ways to keep the creative flow going; maybe it's a regular brainstorming session, a shared document for pitching ideas, or a quick Slack channel where people can drop suggestions. The goal is to create a culture where innovation isn't a one-time event, it's just how your team operates.

When you keep the door open for new ideas, you're setting yourself and your team up to stay agile and ahead of the game, no matter what changes come your way.

## Trust Your Gut

Ever found yourself second-guessing a big decision in the heat of the moment? Trusting your instincts can be a deal breaker for your career. When you have confidence in your abilities, you can make bold, effective choices, even when the path forward isn't clear. The key is stepping outside your comfort zone and making decisions that align with your values and long-term goals. The more you do it, the sharper your instincts become and the more clarity you'll have when tackling tough situations.

Picture this: you're in a high-stakes project meeting, and an unexpected challenge pops up. Instead of freezing or overanalyzing, you trust what you know. You lean on your understanding of the project's goals, your team's strengths, and the real-time data in front of you. You make the call, adjust the strategy as needed, and keep things moving forward.

Building this kind of confidence doesn't happen overnight. Take time to reflect on past wins and challenges, what worked, what didn't, and what you learned. The more you trust yourself, the more others will trust you too. And that kind of decisive leadership? That's what gets noticed when it's time to choose the next CEO.

**Yes, But...**

If you catch yourself saying, "Yes, but..." in a conversation, you might not be truly listening. Strong, flexible communication is one of the most important skills you can have as a leader; it helps you navigate challenges, think on your feet, and keep things moving in the right direction. When you communicate clearly and directly, your team stays on the same page, you can adapt to changes more easily, and you lead with confidence.

As a woman leader, make it a priority to communicate with clarity and purpose. Keep your messages concise and actionable so your team knows exactly what needs to be done. In meetings, lay out goals, expectations, and next steps in a way that's easy to follow. And don't be afraid to use visuals, quick summaries, or check-ins to make sure everyone is on the same page.

For example, in a project kickoff meeting, don't just dive into the details, set the stage. Clearly outline the project's scope, objectives, and deadlines. Invite questions and feedback to make sure everyone is aligned. And beyond meetings, keep communication flowing with emails, memos, or quick status updates to keep everyone informed and focused.

When things get uncertain or change happens fast, communication becomes even more critical. Be open, tackle concerns head-on, and make sure your team knows what's going on. When people feel informed and heard, they stay engaged, motivated, and ready to move forward with you.

**Master the Pivot**

Think about a time when you had everything planned until suddenly, you didn't. Maybe you had clear goals and a solid strategy, and then, out of nowhere, something threw everything off course. During a market shift, a supply chain issue, a leadership change, or whatever it was, you had to figure out how to move forward. That's where real leadership comes in.

Success is knowing when to adjust. The best leaders stay flexible, keep their eyes on the goal, and adapt when challenges arise. When things don't go as expected, open up the conversation, bring in fresh ideas, and collaborate on solutions. A leader who can pivot with confidence earns both trust and respect.

And remember, setbacks aren't failures. They're opportunities to refine your strategy. When things go off track, gather your team, figure out what happened, and pull out the lessons that will make you stronger. Adjust, improve, and turn every challenge into a steppingstone.

Great leaders don't just get through change, they master it. By staying adaptable, you turn roadblocks into breakthroughs, setbacks into strategies, and challenges into fuel for your next big success.

## Who's in Your Corner?

Have you ever faced a tough challenge and realized you didn't have the right people to turn to for advice or support? It's a frustrating feeling, but here's the truth: strong networks and collaboration can be game-changers when you're navigating uncertainty and driving innovation.

Building a solid network is about intentionally connecting with people who challenge and inspire you. Seek out mentors, industry experts, and peers who bring fresh perspectives. Attend conferences, join professional groups, and engage in online communities where real conversations happen. The more diverse your network, the stronger your leadership becomes.

Let's say you're the director of a thriving early childhood education (ECE) center. For years, your program has been built on in-person learning, but suddenly, everything shifts. New policies, AI-driven learning tools, and changing parental preferences for hybrid and remote models start shaking up the industry. Enrollment drops and competition from tech-driven programs heats up.

Instead of panicking, you see this as an opportunity. You turn to your network. First, you reach out to other ECE directors on LinkedIn and through professional groups, joining virtual roundtables to hear how they're adapting. Some have successfully integrated AI-assisted learning tools, while others have launched hybrid, home-based models.

Next, you check in with your mentor, a retired superintendent who's been through major shifts in education. She suggests piloting a small-scale digital learning initiative to keep your center relevant.

You also talk to parents. Their feedback makes it clear they want flexible, high-quality early learning options.

With all these insights, you pivot. You introduce a hybrid learning model that blends in-person and virtual engagement, incorporates AI-driven lesson customization, and offers evening "parent coaching" sessions.

Six months later, your enrollment stabilizes, and your center is now a leader in innovative early learning solutions. All because you tapped into your network, learned from others, and adapted your approach.

That's the power of collaboration.

## PARTING SHOTS

In today's fast-paced world, female leaders are truly making waves by mastering the art of blending preparation with improvisation. Imagine the confidence that comes from being thoroughly prepared yet agile enough to adapt on the fly.

When women leaders stay present and lead with empathy, they can tackle challenges with confidence and grace. Emotional intelligence and strong communication skills are game-changers when it comes to influencing decisions and making an impact.

Even in the face of gender bias, smart leaders know how to use both their voices and their silence strategically. Instead of feeling pressured to always speak up, they choose their moments wisely, making thoughtful contributions that command attention and drive change.

What's remarkable is how these leaders leverage over-preparation alongside their ability to pivot swiftly in unexpected situations. This combination of emotional intelligence and adaptive expertise not only helps them overcome obstacles but also helps them to lead with authority and achieve long-term success in their fields.

Think about how this approach fits into your journey. Balancing preparation with a willingness to adapt can open doors to new opportunities and fresh ideas. As Johnson and Mohr suggest, staying proactive and responsive to the needs of clients, employees, and ever-changing environments can set you apart as a leader. How can you anticipate challenges while staying flexible? The more you embrace this mindset, the stronger and more impactful your leadership will become.

## THOUGHT-PROVOKING REFLECTIONS

### Reflecting on Personal Experiences

*Question*: Reflecting on a time when you had to improvise, how did trusting your knowledge and instincts help you navigate that situation? What did you learn about the balance between preparation and improvisation?

### Applying Lessons to Current Situations

*Question*: In your current role or situation, how can you apply the lessons of blending preparation with improvisation to enhance your ability to adapt and communicate effectively, especially when faced with unexpected challenges?

### Preparing for Future Scenarios

*Question:* Imagine you are leading your team through a major project, and midway through, unexpected challenges arise that require you to pivot quickly. Looking ahead, how would you cultivate a mindset that combines both preparation and adaptability to confidently navigate this dynamic situation? What steps can you take now to develop this ability further, ensuring you can lead effectively when faced with future curveballs?

# CAREER TALK

If you see a better way, speak up. If you have a bold idea, push for it. Leaders don't wait for approval—they create momentum.

## Chapter III

### SHINE BRIGHT
### Find Effective Forms of Self-Promotion

*"Did I promote myself? No, but here's the kicker!
I think the pain, the struggle,
the trauma and the scars of being diminished
because I was a woman caused
me to hide automatically and run from those
opportunities for promotion."*

Many women question why their academic or professional excellence hasn't always led to swift career advancement. W. Johnson and Mohr (2013) explore the complexities of self-promotion, noting that many academically successful women assume their achievements will naturally lead to career success. However, self-promotion remains a challenge for many women, as they often feel their work should speak for itself. This uncertainty can create confusion, as traditional self-promotion strategies may not align with their approach. Instead, Johnson and Mohr suggest that women consider redefining success by focusing on collective achievements, highlighting team wins rather than solely individual accomplishments. This shift allows women to gain recognition while staying true to their values.

Martha Stewart's rise to success exemplifies skillful self-promotion. Beginning her career with a passion for housekeeping, cooking, and entertaining, she effectively marketed her expertise and lifestyle brand. Stewart's breakthrough came with her TV show, "Martha Stewart Living," where she shared practical living tips, cultivating a relatable on-screen persona that resonated with audiences and formed the basis of her self-promotion strategy (Spritz, 1997).

Expanding beyond television, Stewart built a media empire through magazines, publications, and online platforms, leveraging digital channels to engage directly with her audience and promote her brand and products. Her career trajectory underscores how effective self-promotion can lead to significant success, propelling her from an entrepreneur to an internationally recognized lifestyle icon.

Self-promotion can be a double-edged sword for women, especially in male-dominated fields. When done well, it builds confidence, credibility, and career momentum. When mismanaged, it risks backlash or reinforces stereotypes.

A powerful solution? Women supporting each other. Collaborative self-promotion, highlighting team successes, amplifying each other's achievements, and leveraging mentorship help navigate societal expectations while strengthening professional visibility.

However, balance is key. Overemphasizing personal success can sometimes be perceived as self-serving, while under-promoting can lead to being overlooked. The challenge for women leaders is to confidently own their contributions while fostering the trust and collaboration essential for strong leadership.

In the next section, Voices of Power, we'll hear directly from women leaders as they share their personal stories about navigating self-promotion. Their insights reveal how they've balanced self-advocacy with uplifting their teams, offering valuable lessons for navigating this complex terrain.

## VOICES OF POWER

### Women Who Shine Bright

Shari, a seasoned executive, reflects on a common realization among many women in leadership: "Looking back, I realize I didn't promote myself enough throughout my career. I prioritized my work performance, fiscal impact, reputation, and client satisfaction, which are all important, but I now see the value in actively sharing my achievements. Those who effectively self-promote often advance more swiftly in their careers."

Too often, women hesitate to highlight their successes, fearing they'll come across as boastful or overly self-serving. Yet, strategic self-promotion is not just about personal gain, it's about ensuring that hard work and accomplishments are recognized, opening doors to new opportunities. In this section, we explore the challenges many women face in self-promotion, the strategies they've embraced, and how learning to confidently showcase their talents can empower them to take their careers to the next level.

### Flash and Glitter

Many women in our research shared the belief that excessive self-promotion, especially when perceived as contrived, can have a counterproductive effect. They argued that doing excellent work will naturally draw attention, even if one doesn't actively seek it. Most of the women noted that they had observed instances where overt self-promotion turned others off, diminishing the individual's perceived abilities and overall likability.

Alli shared her thoughts on this topic: "The uniqueness and excellence that anyone brings to a leadership role might be noticed through results, but when you deliberately highlight these qualities, it often seems more like an attempt at publicity than a genuine showcase of the organization's achievements."

Interestingly, contrary to much of the conventional advice on self-promotion, many felt that women who focus too intently on self-promotion often do not enhance their organizations. Monica, for instance, reflected on her experience with women administrators who prioritized self-promotion, finding that these individuals frequently failed to deliver quality work, which became evident through their promotional efforts.

Tracy, an aspiring CEO, noted that some individuals produce glossy pamphlets to highlight their achievements. Still, the credibility of these materials was frequently questioned by both their communities and organizational members.

All women noted that for self-promotion to be effective and have a positive impact on one's career, it needed to be in the vein of substance over publicity. One female school superintendent expressed that when self-promotion comes in the form of highlighting student achievement and student programming, it serves the purpose of showcasing the work that happens under the person's leadership. The intentionality of promoting district initiatives, programs, and successes is heightened once one achieves the status of superintendent because the story of the district ultimately tells the story of the leader.

## The Common Good

Balancing self-promotion with humility is a challenge many women navigate. Shari, a Latina executive, stated, "I share my achievements and accomplishments under an air of humility. Humility is a major value in my family. It's always been challenging for me throughout my career to self-promote. It feels like you're bragging about yourself, and that's kind of a hard thing to do."

For example, some women find that their upbringing or cultural norms emphasize working for the collective good rather than highlighting individual accomplishments. "I am Mexicana, Latina, and we're not taught to showcase or show off."

This sentiment was further expressed when one woman said, "And I think it might be a matter of either my culture or even upbringing where we tend to work more toward the common good of the group as opposed to the merit of one person, and we're also taught to be humble."

For women of color, tension is often created between the desire to advance in their careers and the cultural expectation to remain modest. Recognizing and navigating these nuances can help you strike a balance that allows you to confidently showcase your achievements while staying true to your values.

Patty, a successful administrator, discussed how indirect self-promotion often relies on validation from others, noting, "It would be more of a validation of maybe what people have already known or what they've been told." She emphasized humility in her approach, saying, "But I also share my achievements ... under an air of humility."

# CAREER TRUTHS

---

*Your career is not a ladder— it's a jungle gym.*

## Building Bridges

Most of our women leaders in this study agreed that effective forms of self-promotion were most successful when working on relationship building at all levels of the organization. Sarah, a director, shared that self-promotion through relationships was the only appropriate way that she felt she was selling who she was as a person.

Amy, a seasoned administrator, understood that she is the face of her organization and has been for many years. As such, the organization's accomplishments are her own, and the relationships she has formed are part of those accomplishments. Many of these women highlighted the need for self-promotion to drive their organizations forward while emphasizing the importance of promoting others, building relationships, and supporting fellow leaders' growth. It's about expanding the idea of self-promotion beyond just oneself.

For instance, Isabella shared a story about a mentor who once gave her a great idea. She planned to credit the mentor, but they insisted she should take the credit herself because it would benefit her career more. These kinds of relationships have shaped these women's reputations and contributed positively to their careers, becoming integral parts of their professional narratives.

## Sisterhood

It's not uncommon for women to feel a dip in confidence during their careers, especially when female support seems scarce. In such moments, reaching out to other women can be a lifeline, helping to build resilience. One woman leader shared an experience where, in her organization, empowerment and sisterhood were lacking, and another female leader discouraged self-promotion.

This scenario highlights a phenomenon known as "queen bee syndrome," where some women in leadership roles distance themselves from other women to fit into male-dominated environments (Khan, 2023). This behavior can create a culture where self-advocacy is discouraged, making it even more crucial for women to seek out supportive networks. Building connections with like-minded women can foster a sense of community and provide the encouragement needed to navigate challenging workplaces.

The sad thing, however, is that sometimes women don't realize that when one woman advances, it helps break barriers, and if we focus on supporting each other, we can bring more women along.

Self-promotion in the context of empowerment and sisterhood has been more prevalent with church-associated organizations. Before women were ordained in her church, one woman set a goal to build connections at women's and leadership conferences. This approach not only expanded her network but also created opportunities for speaking and discipleship.

*That self-promotion thing can eat at you and break your confidence because you already feel like you're in someone else's locker room, in a sense. You're a female, and you're not supposed to be here. It may be different when you're among many female pastors in a larger church, but in a small church, especially now in a senior pastor role, it's so hard and I constantly remind myself that I am in the right position.*

Remember, seeking support is a strategy for success. By uplifting each other, women can create environments where everyone thrives.

**Looking Back**

Every woman in our study looked back on their career and realized that if they'd embraced self-promotion earlier, they might have climbed the ladder faster. It's common for women to feel uneasy about highlighting their achievements, often due to fears of appearing boastful or facing backlash. However, by confidently showcasing your accomplishments, you not only pave the way for your own advancement but also inspire and empower other women to do the same. One of the most compelling insights came from Rose, a confident female leader, who shared her realization with us:

*If I had been more of a self-promoter, maybe we would have gotten more contracts. However, I still believe in the quality of my work, which speaks for itself. My personality does not lend itself to self-promotion. I have attended national conferences, and many people know me because I have been the only Black woman in my field for a long time. It is not hard to recognize me as a Black woman. People know me because of my work, but they do not know that I am the president of a company unless they research me. None of them knew I owned a company, and I sold it. Perhaps having been more of a self-promoter would have positively impacted my career advancement.*

And another woman revealed, "Showing everything we have done has helped in my promotion. If I stayed super quiet and did not do some of those things, I think I would just get lost in the background, and people would think of me as a worker bee, and they would keep giving me more work, but then I would remain in that position."

## Brag Smart, Win Big

Nearly all the women leaders remarked that effective self-promotion is challenging to master and can even be detrimental if mishandled. However, there was a consensus on one key point: by highlighting their organization's accomplishments, they were also showcasing their own leadership story.

Many school superintendents emphasized the importance of being recognized and visibly connected to their districts. They wanted their leadership to be associated with the district's successes. One seasoned superintendent explained that by actively promoting the district and building strong relationships within the community, leaders not only elevate their schools but also enhance their own professional presence.

All of the women in our study noted that modesty and hesitancy to self-promote were key factors in their decision that their self-promotion would come through accomplishments of the organization rather than actual things they have done. For example, one woman said that when a finger is pointing at her in praise, she routinely points it to someone else.

Latina women leaders talked about how cultural values around humility made direct self-promotion feel uncomfortable.

Instead, they found more subtle ways to highlight their accomplishments. A common theme emerged: rather than boasting about their successes, they let their actions speak for them. Many shared how they stayed actively involved in their communities, whether by attending local meetings or showing up at events like a recent carnival. Their presence didn't go unnoticed; community leaders took the time to recognize their contributions. This approach allowed them to gain visibility and respect without having to self-promote in a way that felt unnatural.

In summary, while the concept of self-promotion can be contentious and culturally complex, effective promotion is often achieved through a combination of showcasing organizational accomplishments, building relationships, and advocating for oneself in a manner that aligns with personal values and cultural norms.

# CAREER TRUTHS

*Playing it safe is the riskiest move you can make.*

## PROMOTIONAL POWER MOVES

The topic of self-promotion among women leaders sparks a range of viewpoints. For some, unabashed self-promotion stands as a crucial tool for gaining visibility and climbing the career ladder. They assert its necessity in a competitive environment where recognition often translates to opportunity. Yet, contrasting voices caution against the perils of excessive self-promotion.

Many leaders recognize that promoting themselves can be a smart career move, but they still feel uneasy about it. This mix of views shows just how complicated self-promotion is in the workplace.

In this section, we'll explore some simple but powerful strategies for self-promotion that strike a balance between confidence and authenticity. By using these approaches, you can steer your career more effectively, making sure you're noticed while staying true to your values. Dive in to discover how to harness the power of self-promotion in a way that works for you!

**Highlight Team Achievements**

Highlighting your team's achievements is a great way to show leadership and teamwork. When you talk about your own role, try to connect it to the team's overall success. For instance, if you're leading a project that boosts your company's profile, don't just focus on what you did. Share how each team member's unique skills and efforts made the project a success. This action not only shows you're a team player but also emphasizes the collective effort behind the achievement.

## Leverage Organizational Wins

Share how your work has contributed to key milestones or goals of the organization. For instance, discuss how a project you led resulted in achieving significant organizational objectives.

## Use Data and Results

Quantify your achievements with concrete data and results. Instead of simply stating that you improved processes, provide specific metrics or outcomes that illustrate the impact of your work.

## Tell Success Stories

Share compelling stories about successful projects or initiatives, emphasizing your role in overcoming challenges and driving results. Use these stories in performance reviews, networking situations, or when discussing your contributions in meetings.

## Seek and Share Testimonials

Encourage colleagues and supervisors to provide testimonials or endorsements of your work. Share these endorsements on professional platforms or in discussions to highlight your positive impact through others' perspectives.

## Position Yourself as a Thought Leader

Contribute to industry discussions or author articles on topics relevant to your field. This strategy positions you as an expert and allows you to showcase your knowledge and insights without directly self-promoting.

**Create a Success Portfolio**

Develop a portfolio or a "brag book" that includes key accomplishments, project summaries, and endorsements. Use it during performance reviews or when seeking new opportunities to provide a well-rounded view of your contributions.

**Mentor and Support Others**

Engage in mentoring or supporting the development of others in your organization. Highlight how you've contributed to their growth and the positive outcomes that resulted from your guidance.

**Be Visible and Accessible**

Attend key meetings, participate in industry events, and engage in conversations that align with your expertise. Being visible in relevant contexts helps others recognize and appreciate your contributions.

## PARTING SHOTS

Reflecting on the journey of self-promotion reveals how closely our firsthand experiences and cultural influences shape this aspect of career growth. Many women, like our featured female pastor, have navigated the challenges of promoting themselves in environments where systemic biases or personal reservations might have overshadowed their achievements. As explored, traditional methods of self-promotion may not always align with our values or resonate with our personal and cultural identities.

It's important to understand that self-promotion isn't a one-size-fits-all strategy. Instead of merely broadcasting personal victories, consider celebrating team successes and the collective achievements of your organization. This approach not only aligns with the principles of strategic self-promotion but also enhances your authenticity and connection with others. Reflecting on figures like Martha Stewart, who built a legacy through a mix of strategic self-promotion and genuine passion, can provide valuable insights into crafting your unique promotional style.

As you move forward, think of self-promotion not just as talking about yourself but as showcasing the impact you make and the value you bring to a greater mission. How can you confidently share your accomplishments while staying true to your values? When you navigate this balance with authenticity, you'll carve out a path to success that feels both meaningful and genuinely yours.

## THOUGHT-PROVOKING REFLECTIONS

### Reflecting on Personal Experiences:

*Question:* Can you recall a time when effectively promoting yourself or increasing your visibility made a positive impact on your goals, and what did you learn from that experience about navigating self-promotion?

### Applying Lessons to Current Situations:

*Question:* How can you apply what you've learned about self-promotion and visibility to enhance your impact and opportunities in your current situation?

### Preparing for Future Scenarios:

*Question:* How can you prepare to effectively promote yourself and increase your visibility in future situations where you need to stand out or advance your goals?

# CAREER TALK

Phrases like "I don't mean to disagree, but..." weaken your influence. Instead, say: "Here's an alternative approach that could work better."

## Chapter IV

### EMBRACE THE UNKNOWN
### Welcome a Less Prescribed Career Path

*"I've done that. I'm just doing the job now. I'm not learning any more, and I need to move on."*

Have you ever thought that the traditional "climb the ladder" career path might not be the only way to reach the top? Imagine this: Georgia, a mid-level manager at a tech firm, decided to take a lateral move to lead a completely different department. At first, her colleagues were puzzled; why step sideways when she could keep climbing? However, Georgia knew that learning the ins and outs of a different part of the company would broaden her perspective and strengthen her leadership skills. Fast forward three years and Georgia's deep understanding of the business has positioned her as the top candidate for an executive role.

Georgia's approach aligns with the research by Johnson and Mohr (2013), which highlights how women who embrace unconventional career moves often leverage their strengths to achieve top positions. Lateral moves, job changes, and even exploring different industries can help women build a unique toolkit of skills, adaptability, and creativity, qualities essential for leadership in today's fast-paced world.

While stepping off the traditional path can feel risky, it also opens doors to unexpected opportunities for growth and innovation. These "zigzag" careers may come with uncertainties, but they also foster resilience and personal development. Women who take these routes often find themselves better prepared to tackle leadership challenges with fresh perspectives and innovative solutions.

## VOICES OF POWER

### Women Who Embrace the Unknown

Our research into women's career journeys has uncovered some fascinating insights. Many women have found that stepping off the traditional career path has led to significant personal and professional growth. From our conversations, a few key themes stood out: being adaptable, always learning, and having the courage to step out of your comfort zone is crucial for success.

### Adapt and Thrive

Women who stay curious and open to learning are better equipped to handle unexpected career twists. When industries shift, those who adapt and embrace new opportunities are the ones who keep moving forward and thriving. For instance, Tanya underscored the necessity of adaptability. As often the only female in the boardroom, she reflected on the predictable nature of the industry as a driver of growth.

> *I would analyze the rapid shifts in the conversation and wait to express my feelings on a topic until the males in the*

> *room had exhausted their opinions, after which someone would ask me for my thoughts. At this point, the attention would be entirely on me, and everyone would be listening. Doing this kept me on my toes and forced me to be innovative and adapt based on what I was hearing. I believe this had a positive impact on my career. Allowing me to build connections and participate in discussions where I could influence decisions was truly a game-changer for me.*

Another female highlighted the personal development she achieved through assessments and learning from varied experiences, showcasing how adaptability enhanced her career trajectory in ways she never thought possible.

> *I was pulled into the administrative team and began to build the ministry. It did not take long for me to join multiple teams and begin to orchestrate and develop training programs to teach and train the board of directors. Over these past years in ministry, I have gone from pastor's assistant to coadministration, an ordained minister, and now I am an ordained pastor, third in command.*

Other women shared how strategic thinking allowed them to thrive by embracing adaptability and flexibility throughout their careers. They recounted experiences such as taking on diverse roles, navigating unexpected situations, and confidently speaking on diverse topics when needed. One woman reflected, "Every day, we're pivoting. No matter how prepared we are, something always gets tossed into the mix. It's about figuring out what's needed and maneuvering."

# CAREER TALK

If It Hasn't Been Done Before, Even Better. Push past expectations, question outdated norms, and take risks others avoid.

## Shifting Gears

How can stepping out of our comfort zones and embracing risk redefine our careers? Our research revealed that taking risks has been a transformative factor for many women's professional journeys.

Kira emphasized the importance of gaining diverse experiences to build credibility. She shared, "I'm a firm believer in experiencing different roles. You build credibility by sitting in multiple seats." Her approach highlights how a varied career path can create a solid foundation for leadership and growth.

Miriam's story reflects a similar pivot. Having worked as an attorney before transitioning to education, she credited her legal background with equipping her to advocate for equity as a superintendent. Her willingness to step into a new field demonstrates the power of transferable skills and embracing change.

Tanya shared a compelling story of challenging the status quo. When her supervisor falsely claimed there was no open position in a different region, Tanya took a chance. She connected with the leadership team, interviewed, and secured the role. Her determination showcases how taking initiative can lead to unexpected opportunities.

For many women, non-traditional career paths were key to their success. Janine reflected on her unconventional journey: "Coming out of a daycare facility, I spent most of my time working with children and helping parents, so starting a church with just family members and a small congregation felt daunting. But I realized that my work with people and processes came organically, even though becoming a minister was never something I aspired to."

Melissa echoed this sentiment, saying, "Taking an unconventional path might not yield immediate rewards, but I believe I wouldn't be where I am today if I hadn't explored new opportunities and accepted a lower position at a different company."

**Knowledge Boost**

Learning and developing new skills emerged as a cornerstone for career advancement. Women's professional growth often stems from acquiring knowledge through education, training, and real-world experience.

Take Nadia, for example. She stepped away from her role as a superintendent to lead a post-secondary degree program. This move allowed her to sharpen her organizational leadership skills by teaching them to others. In the process, she expanded her professional network and built a strong reputation among those who witnessed her work firsthand.

Janel focused on her personal strengths and growth by diving deeply into bilingual special education across multiple school districts. Reflecting on her journey, she shared, "I really do feel I am an expert. I often served as a consultant for other school districts regarding bilingual special education issues." Her story highlights the power of carving out a niche and owning your expertise as a path to professional success.

Then there's Macie, who broadened her skill set by transitioning from curriculum and instruction to human resources. This shift allowed her to develop expertise in legal and programmatic areas she hadn't previously explored, enriching her career trajectory.

## Uncharted Paths

The women we interviewed showed that stepping off the traditional career path and embracing diverse experiences can really boost leadership skills and broaden perspectives. For instance, a study found that 86% of female business leaders credit their success to non-traditional career moves (Blank, 2019).

Peyton shared how an unexpected internship shaped her path. "When I started as a music administrator at a church, I never imagined where it would lead. Shortly after, I was asked to lead the girls in the youth ministry, helping them grow as leaders and, eventually the youth ministry worship team. That's when I discovered my true passion: developing leaders."

Lina highlighted how staying open to new opportunities within her role contributed to her growth. "I'm part of this committee, part of that committee, that's how I learn and grow," she explained. Her willingness to step up in these settings provided invaluable insights and skills that have fueled her career.

Michele's story underscores the power of building skills through hands-on experience. She recounted her time in a corporate quality control role: "In that position, I had to learn how to oversee and improve processes. It completely changed the way I present myself. I realized that leadership isn't about knowing every statistic; it's about how you guide others and bring your ideas to life."

Tina discovered the value of lateral moves and small career shifts. She described working in different states, cities, and even varying types of buildings. "Each new setting was a chance to learn and grow. I didn't just gain technical skills; I built a leadership style that adapts to different environments and challenges."

These women's stories show that great leaders aren't made by following a straight path. Instead, their diverse experiences shape their success. Their message is clear: every step, even the unconventional ones, builds valuable skills and opens new doors.

**Bold Role Shifts**

For many women leaders, the key to career growth lies in seeking out opportunities, embracing nontraditional roles, and proactively shaping their paths. Maritza captured this drive for continuous growth, saying, "I needed to move because, okay, I've done that. I'm just doing the job. I'm not learning anymore, and I need to move on."

Regina's story illustrates the value of stepping into nontraditional roles.

> *A classical music career is quite different; you audition, study the music, complete character studies and staging. But when you step away from what you thought would define your career, you rebuild from the ground up. I went back to being a 24-hour fitness receptionist but I will always be a musician. It was humbling. But it taught me to connect with real people, handle issues, and be present. Then I transitioned into ministry and realized that both experiences prepared me to lead people, own the room, and guide a team.*

Jean's proactive approach underscores the importance of taking initiative. She recalled a pivotal moment when she challenged her manager to support her move to a higher position in another state. "I realized that if I didn't make the first move, my manager would never let me go because I was so good at my current role. That was my first real step toward advancing in my career."

Celene spoke about the challenges of gaining promotions and the value of stepping down to move forward. "I moved from a national role to a local position, and while it felt like a step back, it gave me a broader perspective and added credibility. Sitting in that seat taught me so much. When I returned to the national team, I had more influence because I had done the work firsthand."

Another example is Tabitha, who left a district she had spent all her career with for a promotion in another local school district. She left knowing that she would have the opportunity to gain a wider view of the educational landscape and a unique way of leading. In taking on a new perspective she has experienced successes in her transition and has been able to be seen by a different group of potential sponsors and mentors as she moves along in her career.

Seizing opportunities, even unconventional ones, can be transformative. Whether it's moving laterally, stepping into a new field, or advocating for advancement, these women show how embracing change and owning their journeys have propelled them to greater success.

## CAREER TRUTHS

*If you don't ask, the answer is always no.*

## PROMOTIONAL POWER MOVES

In today's ever-evolving professional world, women are boldly redefining what success looks like by embracing diverse career paths and unconventional experiences. These journeys are about discovering new opportunities for growth, building resilience, and advancing in ways that feel authentic and empowering.

What's the secret? Stay adaptable, keep learning, and step outside your comfort zone. Every twist brings a chance to grow, gain confidence, and open new doors. Taking smart risks, whether switching roles, exploring new fields, or tackling big projects can lead to amazing opportunities.

Identifying unconventional career opportunities can be a game-changer for your professional growth. Staying alert and ready to act when unique chances come your way is key. Here's how to stay prepared:

### Reflect on Your Passions and Strengths

Think about what you're genuinely interested in and where your skills lie. Unconventional careers often align closely with personal passions and unique abilities. For example, if you love storytelling and technology, a career in virtual reality content creation might be a fit.

### Explore Emerging Industries

Stay informed about new and growing industries. Fields like renewable energy, biotechnology, and remote work solutions are evolving rapidly and offer unconventional opportunities. Reading industry reports, news articles, and trend analyses can help you spot these areas.

### Network with Diverse Professionals

Connect with people outside your usual circles. Attend industry meetups, conferences, and online forums. Networking can reveal less obvious career paths and give you insights into emerging roles that aren't widely known yet.

### Consider Lateral Moves

Look at opportunities within your current organization or field that might not be on the traditional career ladder but offer new challenges and growth. Lateral moves can provide a broader perspective and lead to unexpected leadership roles.

### Research Non-Traditional Roles

Investigate roles that don't fit the typical job descriptions you're familiar with. Jobs like UX researcher, digital nomad, or sustainability consultant may not be on every job board but they are increasingly in demand.

### Leverage Online Resources

Use platforms like LinkedIn, job boards, and industry-specific websites to search for unusual roles or startups. Websites like Glassdoor and Indeed often list unique positions that may not be immediately obvious.

### Think Outside the Box

Consider how your current skills could be applied in new ways. For instance, a background in marketing could translate into a role in data analytics or a non-profit organization.

### Experiment with Freelancing or Side Projects

Taking on freelance projects or starting a side business can open up unconventional opportunities and help you discover new career interests. It also provides practical experience in emerging fields.

### Stay Open-Minded and Flexible

Keep a mindset open to change and exploration. Unconventional opportunities often require a willingness to adapt and try new things.

## PARTING SHOTS

As we conclude this chapter by embracing the unknown and navigating a flexible career journey, consider this: Are you ready to redefine your path and seize new opportunities? The experiences shared by women who ventured off the beaten track reveal a powerful truth: Success often lies beyond conventional routes. By embracing risk, adapting to change, and committing to continual learning, you can unlock new doors and elevate your career.

Take a moment to think about what excites you. What industries spark your curiosity? What unconventional roles play to your strengths? Every bold step, even the ones that feel like detours, adds depth to your journey and prepares you for bigger opportunities. How can you challenge yourself to think beyond the traditional path? As you move forward, trust that embracing the unknown can lead to some of your greatest successes.

## THOUGHT-PROVOKING REFLECTIONS

### Reflecting on Personal Experiences

*Question*: How has embracing uncertainty and taking bold steps in your career path led to unexpected growth and opportunities you might never have considered?

### Applying Lessons to Current Situations

*Question*: What steps can you take today to embrace uncertainty in your career and turn potential challenges into opportunities for growth and reinvention?

### Preparing for Future Scenarios

*Question:* How can you proactively build skills and mindset strategies to navigate and thrive in future career shifts or unexpected changes?

# CAREER TALK

Success feels uncomfortable—that means you're growing. If your career feels too easy, you're not stretching enough.

## Chapter V

### RESPECT ABOVE ALL
### Aim for Being Respected, Not Just Liked

*"At first, it was important for me to be liked.
As I became more experienced, it was more important to be respected."*

Let's talk about a common dilemma many of us face in our professional lives: balancing being liked with being respected. It's a tightrope walk, isn't it? On the one hand, we want to be authentic and true to ourselves; on the other, we're aware of societal expectations and the fear of being labeled as too assertive or, conversely, too accommodating.

Research reveals a troubling reality. As women climb the ladder of success, they become less liked by both men and women (Curmudgeon Group, 2020). Unfortunately, this harsh bias can push women away from certain fields or leadership roles altogether, forcing them to weigh success against social acceptance.

Think about the moments when you've dared to step off the well-trodden path and make a bold, unexpected choice. According to Johnson and Mohr (2013), shaking up the status quo often means prioritizing respect over likability, a concept that may feel counterintuitive for many women. We're often conditioned to value harmony and connection. Yet, those who shift their focus toward earning respect rather than seeking approval frequently find themselves breaking barriers and achieving remarkable career milestones.

Striving for respect, not just popularity, means prioritizing professional integrity over being well-liked. It involves making decisions and taking actions that earn the esteem of colleagues and superiors, even if they're not always the easiest or most popular choices (Johnson & Mohr, 2013; J. C. Williams, n.d.). Prioritizing professional respect demonstrates a commitment to upholding high ethical standards and integrity, which might involve making tough calls, like speaking out against injustice or challenging the status quo. However, earning respect through one's actions builds a solid foundation of credibility and trust, which are crucial for long-term success in any professional setting (Eisenbeiss et al., 2008).

In school, popularity often takes precedence, but in the professional realm, earning respect through actions and decisions is paramount. According to Johnson and Mohr (2013), it's more important for women to be respected than simply liked. To pursue their professional goals, women need to set aside popular opinion and focus on building a solid reputation and gaining the trust of their colleagues and superiors. By doing so, women can establish themselves as credible and trustworthy professionals, paving the way for long-term success and recognition in their chosen fields.

Indra Nooyi is well-recognized for her leadership approach, which values respect over popularity, especially during her tenure as CEO of PepsiCo. Indra Nooyi's leadership style blends visionary thinking, emotional intelligence, inclusivity, and accountability. Throughout her career, Nooyi prioritized long-term success, diversity, and integrity, fostering a culture of collaboration while making decisive, compassionate, and ethical decisions.

As Nooyi put it,

*It's really important for women to understand that it's okay to be disliked as long as you're not disrespectful. It's okay to be tough and direct. People will respect you for it. I've always felt that being liked is not as important as being respected. As a leader, you cannot please everyone. You have to make decisions that are right for the business, and you have to accept that some people will not like you for it (BrainyQuote).*

Understanding the distinction between behaviors exhibited by leaders who prioritize being liked versus those who seek to be respected is crucial for effective leadership. The following table contrasts these behaviors, highlighting how each approach influences leadership dynamics.

| Leaders Who Want to Be Liked | Leaders Who Want to Be Respected |
|---|---|
| Seek positive attention and approval | Tell the truth, even if it's unpopular |
| Engage in gossip rather than giving direct feedback | Explain their thinking behind difficult decisions |
| Try to please everyone | Acknowledge issues openly, even if they can't fix them |
| Make promises they can't keep | Say no when necessary |
| Keep strong opinions to themselves | Be open-minded and decisive |
| Flood people with compliments and praise | Give credit when due and accept it themselves |
| Play favorites (but pretend they don't) | Tolerate feelings of disappointment, frustration, sadness, and anger in themselves and others |
| Use information as leverage, withholding or giving it away | Hold people accountable for their results |
| Assign tasks people enjoy rather than challenging assignments | Be consistent and fair in setting rules and expectations |
| Focus more on how people feel about them than on achieving outcomes | Set and honor boundaries for themselves and others |
| (Not included in "liked" section) | Deliver negative feedback directly and promptly |
| | Regularly seek feedback and act on it |
| | Apologize when making mistakes and move on |
| | Model the behavior they expect from others |

Note: Adapted from "Why the Most Successful Leaders Don't Care About Being Liked: Being Liked is Fleeting. Here's What Matters More," by D. G. Riegel, 2018, Inc.

# CAREER TRUTHS

*Confidence isn't knowing all the answers—it's trusting yourself to find them.*

## VOICES OF POWER

### Prioritizing Respect Over Likability

Navigating challenging situations often requires women to balance the delicate line between earning respect and maintaining likability. Many women shared that making tough decisions may not always win approval, but it does earn respect. Equally important, they emphasized the value of maintaining respect through open communication and a composed demeanor, even in the face of disagreement.

In this section, join some women leaders who share their firsthand experiences and insights on navigating these complexities, offering valuable lessons on striking this balance in their leadership journeys.

### Hard Calls, High Stakes

Noelle, a senior leader in a school district, shared an example of addressing performance issues head-on to benefit both staff and students. She described a challenging meeting with a group of administrators where she had to be honest about the need for improvement. "The student scores just weren't where they needed to be," she explained, "and both the district and the board expected progress." While delivering this message initially caused some tension and made her less popular, setting clear expectations earned her respect and strengthened her credibility as a leader.

Reina also shared her perspective on making tough calls in the best interest of students. "I will make hard decisions for the kids," she said, emphasizing her commitment to putting students' needs above all else, even when it's not easy.

Similarly, in the corporate world, female CEOs have demonstrated the importance of making tough decisions for long-term success. For instance, Marissa Mayer, appointed as Yahoo's CEO in 2012 during a period of significant decline, faced the challenge of revitalizing the company (Hartung, 2014). She implemented a series of bold strategies, including overhauling the company's culture and acquiring new businesses, aiming to steer Yahoo toward growth. While some decisions were met with resistance and controversy, Mayer's commitment to making hard calls underscored her focus on the company's long-term viability over short-term popularity.

**Rooted in Respect, Driven by Purpose**

For the women leaders we interviewed, integrity and professionalism far outweighed the importance of being liked. While being liked can be nice, many emphasized that earning trust and respect through ethical decisions and a genuine commitment to their roles mattered much more.

One director explained how building personal connections and showing authentic care for employees fosters respect. Sharon shared an inspiring example: "I know the names of all 300 of my employees." She believes that cultivating relationships and showing care has been the key to being seen as not just likable but genuinely respected.

Evelyn offered another perspective, pointing out that leaders who fail to prioritize personal connections often struggle with both likability and respect. "I've seen directors and superintendents who don't take the time to connect with people, and it shows," she said.

These insights highlight that true leadership isn't just about being liked; it's about earning respect through integrity, professionalism, and meaningful relationships.

## Talk Straight

Open communication and transparency were identified as key factors in earning respect. One senior leader mentioned that being vulnerable and transparent about challenges helped build empathy and support among colleagues, fostering respect and collaboration.

Yana demonstrated her commitment to keeping stakeholders informed, even during tough circumstances, ensuring transparency throughout the process. She illustrated this with her experience in school negotiations and consolidation processes: "We've had very difficult negotiations ... and are going to be going through the school consolidation process now. ... No one can say they didn't know because we've been putting it out there."

## Win Hearts Without Losing Ground

The women in our study reflected on the delicate balance between respect and likability, acknowledging that not everyone will approve of their decisions. They shared how maintaining integrity and making principled choices often earn long-term respect, even if it comes at the cost of initial popularity.

Tina, who works in a male-dominated industry, spoke about the challenges she faces daily. She stressed the importance of standing firm on doing the right thing, regardless of whether it makes her popular. "I'm challenged daily, especially as a woman surrounded by so many men in the industry. I think it's about doing the right thing and expecting the same from others. That's what earns respect." Tina's approach includes setting clear boundaries and expectations, showing that she values fairness over being liked.

Celene echoed this sentiment, admitting, "I know I'm not always well-liked by everyone around me. But I'm confident I'm respected because I approach situations with honesty, fairness, and facts." For her, earning respect through integrity and accuracy takes precedence over popularity or even career advancement.

**Respect Lasts**

Many women emphasized the importance of strategic decision-making for career growth, pointing out that earning respect through honest and thoughtful choices is far more valuable than striving to be universally liked. They shared how prioritizing respect has not only advanced their careers but also reinforced their credibility.

Denise opened up about the challenges of navigating this balance. "I don't see myself acting to be respected or liked," she explained. "My decisions are guided by doing what's right for the business and achieving the results we're aiming for." She emphasized that focusing on strategic decision-making has been key to her professional growth, even when those decisions weren't always popular.

Vicky spoke passionately about the power of respect.

*We all want to own the room," she said. "We want people to enjoy our presence, laugh at our jokes, and feel comfortable around us. But at the end of the day, being liked doesn't compare to being deeply respected. Respect is earned when your word becomes your bond, when it stands strong against fleeting emotions, cultural trends, or the tough calls that come with leadership. For me, respect is the highest form of esteem, built on unwavering trust. Personal opinions may shift, but respect lasts.*

Maddey highlighted the role of credibility in decision-making, emphasizing that data-driven insights have been pivotal to her growth. "Data isn't about opinion, it's about truth," she explained. "When you ground your decisions in data, you eliminate guesswork and personal biases. Throughout my career, I've relied on data not just as a tool, but as a strategic guide that cuts through noise and ensures clarity in every decision."

These insights remind us that as women in leadership, aiming for respect over popularity isn't about sacrificing relationships, it's about building trust and credibility that stand the test of time.

## Defy the Odds, Not the Rules

Many of the women leaders we interviewed shared how they've learned to respectfully challenge authority when necessary, showing assertiveness and confidence in their convictions. They emphasized that delivering feedback or dissent professionally and with facts rather than emotions helps earn respect and build credibility in the workplace.

Tanya reflected on her consistent approach to questioning authority with respect throughout her career. "I've always kept that mentality, questioning respectfully, whether it's an authority figure or not," she said. Her approach demonstrates the power of maintaining professionalism while standing firm in her beliefs.

# CAREER TRUTHS

*Overthinking is the enemy of action.*

Melissa shared how she confidently offers alternative perspectives when she sees better ways to approach a challenge. "I often feel the need to challenge how others think and share my perspective because I usually have a couple of better ways if not just a better way to tackle the issue," she explained.

Celene highlighted the importance of thoughtful pushback, sharing how she's developed confidence over her career by learning to express disagreement respectfully and engage in meaningful conversations. "I've learned that people appreciate thoughtful pushback," she said. "It's about using facts, not feelings, to present your opinion well and diplomatically."

Francisca shared her belief in the importance of fair compensation. "I firmly believe that anyone who provides a service should be compensated for it," she said. As she progressed in her career, she often faced expectations to take on additional tasks beyond her job description without corresponding pay increases. Recognizing the importance of fair compensation, she began to advocate for herself, even though such actions were often met with resistance. By confidently asserting her worth and negotiating for equitable pay, she not only secured the compensation she deserved but also reinforced her self-value and set a precedent for others in her organization. Her experience mirrors the broader challenges many women encounter in the workplace, where advocating for equal pay remains a critical issue.

These stories show that challenging ideas or authority doesn't have to come at the expense of professionalism. By pairing confidence with respect and focusing on constructive dialogue, women can make their voices heard while building trust and respect in their workplaces.

## PROMOTIONAL POWER MOVES

Striking the right balance between respect and likability isn't always easy, but the most successful women know that earning respect comes first. They use smart strategies to navigate this dynamic, ensuring they're seen as both strong and approachable. Here's how they do it:

### Learn to Communicate Clearly

To successfully balance respect and likability, start by setting clear expectations. Communicate your goals and boundaries openly and directly, ensuring that others understand where you stand. This clarity helps to minimize misunderstandings and fosters an atmosphere of mutual respect.

Make active listening a habit. Really hear people out, show you value their input, and take their concerns seriously. Even if you don't always agree, this builds trust and stronger connections. When you listen with intention and lead with authenticity, you'll navigate challenges with confidence and earn both respect and meaningful relationships along the way.

### Maintain Consistency and Uphold Integrity

Stay true to your values. Clearly define your principles and let them guide your actions and decisions, even when facing criticism or unpopularity. Consistency in upholding your values will reinforce your integrity and build trust. Additionally, practice giving honest, constructive feedback.

Give honest, helpful feedback that's both direct and thoughtful. There's no need to sugarcoat just to keep everyone happy. When you stay authentic and fair, you build respect while keeping strong, professional relationships intact.

## Empathize and Understand

Begin by showing empathy. Take the time to understand others' emotions and viewpoints, acknowledging their feelings even when you need to stand firm in your own standards. Demonstrating this level of understanding fosters trust and connection while maintaining your integrity. Additionally, actively support your colleagues and team members.

Encourage, support, and recognize others, even when tough decisions must be made. Showing empathy and offering genuine help builds strong, respectful relationships that can weather challenges and create a positive, productive workplace.

## Act Professionally and Ensure Fairness

Maintain clear professional boundaries. Keep interactions respectful and focused, ensuring that personal likability never compromises your ability to treat others fairly and equitably. Next, engage in fair decision-making. Base your decisions on what is just and beneficial for the greater good rather than seeking to win approval.

Tackle challenges with a clear head, focusing on what's fair and necessary, not just what's popular. When you lead with professionalism and integrity, you build trust and earn respect that truly lasts.

## Learn to Adapt and Be Resilient

Address conflicts directly and respectfully. Approach disagreements with a balanced mindset, focusing on resolving issues without alienating others. By maintaining respect during tough conversations, you can preserve relationships while managing differing opinions. Additionally, cultivate resilience.

Stay true to what you believe in, even when it's not the popular choice. Stand your ground with confidence but stay open to feedback that helps you grow. Holding firm to your values isn't just a sign of strength; it's how you earn real respect that lasts.

## Build Trust and Cultivate Rapport

Develop trust. Be reliable by following through on your commitments and consistently meeting expectations. Demonstrating dependability fosters trust, which is essential for earning respect and makes your interactions smoother and more positive.

Connect with your colleagues in an authentic way. Listen, show interest, and value their ideas. Genuine relationships make it easier to earn respect while staying approachable, creating a solid foundation for teamwork and success.

## Balance Firmness with Approachability

Aim to be approachable yet firm. Start by being friendly and open, creating an environment where others feel comfortable sharing their thoughts and ideas. At the same time, maintain authority by clearly communicating your expectations and standing by your decisions. This combination of approachability and firmness ensures that you remain accessible while earning respect for your clarity and leadership.

When you mix these strategies, you don't have to choose between being respected and being liked, you can have both. Stay true to your values while building strong, positive relationships, and you'll earn the respect you deserve without sacrificing connection.

## PARTING SHOTS

In the journey toward professional success, prioritizing respect over mere likability emerges as a crucial strategy. As we've explored, earning respect often involves making difficult choices and standing firm in your principles, even when it's challenging. Angela Merkel's steadfast leadership and Margaret Thatcher's emphasis on integrity over popularity underscore the power of this approach.

As you move forward, consider how focusing on respect can reshape your career path. Reflect on moments when prioritizing integrity might have led to more profound respect from colleagues and superiors. How can you incorporate these lessons into your daily professional interactions?

Looking ahead, think about how you can navigate future challenges with a balance of firmness and approachability. Are there upcoming decisions where focusing on respect could enhance your long-term success and credibility?

When it comes down to it, building a successful career with integrity and impact starts with earning respect. As you navigate your own path, think about how you want to be known, not just for what you achieve but for the principles you stand by. What kind of legacy do you want to have? Real success comes from staying true to your values, earning respect through action, and leading with authenticity.

## THOUGHT-PROVOKING REFLECTIONS

### Reflecting on Personal Experiences

*Question:* How has your perspective on being liked versus being respected evolved over time, and what impact has that shift had on your personal or professional growth?

### Applying Lessons to Current Situations

*Question:* How can you prioritize earning respect over seeking likability in your current situation, and what steps can you take to challenge the status quo and advance in your career?

### Preparing for Future Scenarios

*Question:* How can you apply the balance between earning respect and being liked to prepare for a future situation where you'll need to challenge the status quo or make a bold career decision? Demonstrate this by preparing a future scenario.

# Lasting Impressions

## Collective Power

No two career journeys look the same, and that's what makes them so powerful. Across industries, backgrounds, and experiences, one thing is clear: women have the resilience, intelligence, and drive to lead and succeed, even in spaces that once seemed off-limits. But let's be real—the road isn't always smooth. Systemic barriers, outdated expectations, and personal challenges still show up. So, how do we keep pushing forward? How do we turn those obstacles into steppingstones? That's the conversation worth having.

This book is not just a guide, it is a call to action. It is built on the stories and wisdom of women who have dared to disrupt norms and reimagine what leadership can look like. From education and property management to faith-based leadership, the strategies outlined here are not confined by industry or circumstance. They are designed to empower all women, offering a roadmap to navigate challenges and embrace opportunities with confidence and purpose.

The women whose voices echo throughout these pages remind us of the power of preparation and improvisation, the importance of influence over authority, and the necessity of prioritizing respect over mere likeability. They teach us that while self-promotion may feel uncomfortable, celebrating the collective achievements of teams and communities is a form of leadership in its own right.

Together, these strategies demonstrate that leadership is not about fitting into a mold but about breaking free from it. It's about leveraging the unique perspectives and strengths that women bring to the table, about creating spaces where diverse voices are heard, and about lifting as we climb.

In closing, we hope this book equips and inspires you to disrupt, to challenge, and to rise. The work is not easy, but it is necessary. Whether you are just beginning your career, seeking the next level of leadership, or supporting others along their journey, remember progress is made by those who dare to believe that they are the right person for the job, because they are.

The time for waiting is over. The time for women to lead boldly, unapologetically, and authentically is now. Let's seize it together.

# Your Promotion Power Playbook

## A Bold Strategy for Career Disruption

Congratulations! You've absorbed the disruptive career strategies in Promotion Power. Now it's time to put them into action. This action plan is designed to help you take control of your career trajectory and step into your power.

Use this guide to map out your next bold career moves and keep yourself accountable.

| STEP 1: Identify Your Disruption Zone | |
|---|---|
| What's the biggest career challenge I need to disrupt? (Example: "I always wait for opportunities instead of seeking them out." OR "I shrink myself in meetings.") | |
| **STEP 2: Take a Bold Leap** | |
| What is one risk I will take in the next 30 days? (Example: "Ask for a high-profile project." OR "Pitch myself for a leadership role.") Set a deadline for this action. | |
| **STEP 3: Build Your Power Network** | |
| Who will I seek mentorship from? (List one or two people who can guide, inspire, or advocate for you. They can be mentors, colleagues, or role models.) How will I reach out to them? (Email, coffee chat, LinkedIn, etc.) (Example: "I will message my former boss on LinkedIn by next Friday.") | |

| | |
|---|---|
| **STEP 4:** **Amplify Your Voice** | |
| One way I will advocate for myself this year: (Example: "Negotiate my salary confidently." OR "Speak up in meetings instead of second-guessing myself.") | |
| **STEP 5:** **Own Your Success** | |
| List three achievements I will celebrate this year: (Too often, we move on to the next goal without celebrating our wins— big or small. Write down your successes and honor them. Think about how you will effectively self-promote and let others know about your accomplishments. | |
| **STEP 6:** **Commit to Disruptive Action** | |
| Write a note to yourself about WHY you are committed to these actions: "I am committed to stepping into my power because..." | |
| **FINAL STEP** **Make It Real** | |
| Snap a picture of this page or rewrite it in your journal. Keep it where you can see it! Challenge yourself to check back in 3 months— what have you accomplished? What needs adjusting? Keep pushing forward! | |

# CAREER TRUTHS

*If they call you 'too much,' they weren't ready for you.*

# REFERENCES

American Bar Association (ABA). (2023). ABA Profile of the Legal Profession. Retrieved from https://www.americanbar.org/data-reports

Association of American Medical Colleges (AAMC). (2023). Physician Specialty Data Report. Retrieved from https://www.aamc.org/data-reports

Association for Psychological Science. (2015, January 20). Women face backlash for speaking up at work. https://www.psychologicalscience.org/news/minds-business/women-face-backlash-for-speaking-up-at-work.html

Ariella, S. (2023, June 8). 25 women in leadership statistics [2023]: Facts on the gender gap in corporate and political leadership. *Zippia*. https://www.zippia.com/advice/women-in-leadership-statistics/

Blank, A. (2019, April 28). Female leaders take non-traditional career paths, study says: How you can, too. Forbes. https://www.forbes.com/sites/averyblank/2019/04/28/female-leaders-take-non-traditional-career-paths-study-says-how-you-can-too/

Brahma, S., Nwafor, C., & Boateng, A. (2021). Board gender diversity and firm performance: The UK evidence. *International Journal of Finance & Economics, 26*(4), 5704–5719.

BrainyQuote. (n.d.). *Indra Nooyi quotes*. BrainyQuote. https://www.brainyquote.com/authors/indra-nooyi-quotes

Curmudgeon Group. (2020, February 27). *Super woman*. Retrieved from https://curmudgeongroup.co/likeability-leadership-the-female-double-bind/

Cursa. (n.d.). *Case studies of successful leadership*. Cursa. Retrieved from https://cursa.app/en/page/case-studies-of-successful-leadership

Eisenbeiss, S. A., Knippenberg, D. V., & Boerner, S. (2008). Transformational leadership and team innovation: Integrating team climate principles. *Journal of Applied Psychology*, *93*(6), 1438–1446.

Eagly, A. H., Johannesen-Schmidt, M. C., & van Engen, M. L. (2003). Transformational, transactional, and laissez-faire leadership styles: A meta-analysis comparing women and men. *Psychological Bulletin*, *129*(4), 569–591. https://doi.org/10.1037/0033-2909.129.4.569

Fast Company. (2024, August 23). Just 6% of CEOs are women worldwide. Retrieved from https://www.fastcompany.com/91177619/just-6-of-ceos-are-women-worldwide?utm_source=chatgpt.co

Feld, K. M. (2021, July 29). Ten female leaders offer advice on how to pivot to new opportunity amidst uncertainty. *Entrepreneur*. https://www.entrepreneur.com/growing-a-business/10-female-leaders-offer-advice-on-how-to-pivot-to-new/365903

Fry, R. (2022, September 26). Women now outnumber men in the US college-educated labor force. Pew Research Center. https://www.pewresearch.org/short-reads/2022/09/26/women-now-outnumber-men-in-the-u-s-college-educated-labor-force/

Garson, H. S. (2011). *Oprah Winfrey: A biography*. Bloomsbury Publishing.

Gray, K. (2018, June 9). Six rewarding reasons to choose a non-traditional career path. Brit + Co. https://www.brit.co/advantages-of-choosing-non-traditional-career-path/

Hartung, A. (2015, December 6). *How bad leadership doomed Yahoo: CEO mistakes are costly*. Forbes. https://www.forbes.com/sites/adamhartung/2015/12/06 how-bad-leadership-doomed-yahoo-ceo-mistakes-are-costly/

Hinchliffe, E. (2024, June 4). Women run just 10.4% of Fortune 500 companies. *Fortune*. Retrieved https://finance.yahoo.com/news/share-fortune-500-companies-run-113000264.html

Johnson, W. (2015). *Disrupt yourself: Putting the power of disruptive innovation to work.* Bibliomotion.

Johnson, W. (2019). *Disrupt yourself: Master relentless change and speed up your learning curve.* Harvard Business Press.

Johnson, W., & Mohr, T. (2019). Disrupt yourself and the way you work. In Harvard Business Review (Ed.), *HBR guide for women at work.* Harvard Business Review Press.

Johnson, W. (2016, January 5). Surfing the S-curve: How to disrupt yourself and why. Lean In. https://leanin.org/news-inspiration/surfing-the-s-curve-how-to-disrupt-yourself-and-why#!

Khan, R. (2023, December 4). Queen bee phenomenon: Myth or reality. SHRM. https://www.shrm.org/in/topics-tools/news/blogs/queen-bee-phenomenon--myth-or-reality

Kowalski, T. J., & Brunner, C. C. (2020). *The American Superintendent: 2020 Decennial Study.* American Association of School Administrators.

Liedtke, M. (2012, July 16). Yahoo names Marissa Mayer CEO. *The Huffington Post.* Retrieved from https://www.huffpost.com/entry/marissa-mayer-yahoo-ceo_n_1679466

Mannucci, P. V., Orazi, D. C., & de Valck, K. (2021, March 11). Improvisation takes practice. *Harvard Business Review.* https://hbr.org/2021/03/improvisation-takes-practice

MarketWatch. (2024, October 21). Why women CEOs are 45% more likely to get fired than men. Retrieved from https://www.morningstar.com/news/marketwatch/20241026271/why-women-ceos-are-45-more-likely-to-get-fired-than-men

Mayberry, M. (2016, April 22). By failing to prepare, you are indeed preparing to fail. *Entrepreneur.* https://www.entrepreneur.com/leadership-by-failing-to-prepare-you-are-indeed-preparing-to-fail/274494

National Association of Women Law Enforcement Executives (NAWLEE). (2023). Women Chiefs in Police Departments Statistics. Retrieved from https://www.nawlee.org/statistics

Novotney, A. (2023, March 23). Women leaders make work better. Here's the science behind how to promote them. https://www.apa.org/topics/women-girls/female-leaders-make-work-better

National School Boards Association. (2020, October 1). Gender gap at the top: Creating the best pipeline for senior leadership means encouraging women to apply. *NSBA*. Retrieved from https://www.nsba.org

Nooyi, I. (2018). My life in full: Work, family, and our future. Portfolio. PBS New Hour, 2015), When will there be enough women on the Supreme Court? Justice Ginsburg answers that question https://www.pbs.org/newshour/show/justice-ginsburg-enough-women-supreme-court?utm_source=chatgpt.com

Reynolds, P. (2011, July). *Women don't self-promote, but maybe they should*. Harvard Division of Continuing Education. https://professional.dce.harvard.edu/blog/women-dont-self-promote-but-maybe-they-should/

Riegel, D. G. (2018, October 18). Why the most successful leaders don't care about being liked: Being liked is fleeting. Here's what matters more. *Inc*. https://www.inc.com/deborah-grayson-riegel/why-most-successful-leaders-dont-care-about-being-liked.html

Salinas, G. (2020, November 25). The armor of a personal brand for women leaders. *IE Insights*. https://www.ie.edu/insights/articles/the-armor-of-a-personal-brand-for-women-leaders/

Samit, J. (2015). *Disrupt You!* Flatiron Books.

Sandberg, S. (2015). *Lean in: Women, work and the will to lead*. Knopf.

School Superintendents Association (AASA). (2023). *The Study of the American Superintendent*. Retrieved from https://www.aasa.org/research

Spitz, E. (1997). *Entertaining: The story of Martha Stewart's rise to fame*. Random House.

Thatcher, M. (n.d.). "If you just set out to be liked, you would be prepared to compromise on anything at any time, and you would achieve nothing." Attributed quote. As quoted in *The Downing Street Years* (1993). HarperCollins.

U.S. Census Bureau. (2023). Educational Attainment in the United States: 2022. Retrieved from https://www.census.gov/data

Williams, J. C. (n.d.). *Why women have to fight to be respected and liked at work* [Video]. Lean In. https://leanin.org/education/what-works-for-women-at-work-part-2-the-tightrope

Zenger, J., & Folkman, J. (2019). Women score higher than men in most leadership skills. *Harvard Business Review*, *92*(10), 86–93.

# CAREER TALK

Perfect Plans Don't Exist —Adaptability Wins! The most successful women aren't just prepared—they're quick on their feet.

## ADAPTATIONS

This section acknowledges sources that served as foundational material for the ideas, frameworks, and insights presented in this book. The content in *Promotion Power* includes adaptations from four doctoral dissertations and two previously published books by one of the authors. Adaptation, in this context, refers to the process of drawing upon original research, themes, and concepts from these works and reinterpreting them for broader application and accessibility in this book.

Green, N. (2024). The use of personal disruption strategies by female executive ministry leaders for career advancement (Doctoral dissertation, University of Massachusetts Global). Digital Commons @ UMass Global. https://digitalcommons.umassglobal.edu/edd_dissertations/550

Hernandez, D. (2024). Personal disruption strategies used by Latina superintendents for career advancement (Doctoral dissertation, University of Massachusetts Global). Digital Commons @ UMass Global. https://digitalcommons.umassglobal.edu/edd_dissertations/542

Oliver, L. (2024). The use of personal disruption strategies by female executives in the property management industry for career advancement (Doctoral dissertation, University of Massachusetts Global). Digital Commons @ UMass Global. https://digitalcommons.umassglobal.edu/edd_dissertations/543

Ryder, M., & Briles, J. (2003). *The sexx factor: Breaking the unwritten codes that sabotage personal and professional lives.* New Horizon Press.

Ryder, M., & Thompson, J. (2022). *Self-sabotage: Ten personal power tips to be your best self on a good day.* Delmar Publishing.

Thompson, T. (2023). Personal disruption strategies used by K-12 female superintendents for career advancement (Doctoral dissertation, University of Massachusetts Global). Digital Commons @ UMass Global. https://digitalcommons.umassglobal.edu/edd_dissertations/533

# CAREER TRUTHS

*Bragging? No. Owning your success? Absolutely.*

# ABOUT THE AUTHORS

**LORRI GOLDMANN, Ed.D.** vice president of diversity and inclusion, is a reliable rainmaker known for her reliability and purpose-driven approach to leadership. With over two decades of experience in the property management industry, she has established herself as a trusted expert and a natural leader who guides, mentors, and motivates others. She is an esteemed and sought-after speaker who consistently delivers impactful presentations on DEI, leadership, mental health, and sales. Her dedication to mentorship, community involvement, and teamwork further highlights her passion for giving back and supporting the growth of others, the industry, and her community. She has mentored countless professionals, helping them navigate their careers, develop essential skills, and achieve their professional aspirations. Dr. Goldmann's accomplishments are vast and varied. She has been featured in several industry magazines, Avenue5 Residential 2019 Corbie Award Winner and 2023 Black Leadership Award Winner. She is a Southern California Rental Housing Association board member, California Real Estate Broker, Chair of the National Apartments Association DEI Strategic Committee, and holds a certificate in Diversity, Equity, and Inclusion in the Workplace from the University of South Florida. Dr. Goldmann is dedicated to ensuring that diversity, equity, and inclusion are prioritized in the property management industry's evolution.

**NEKO COLEMAN GREEN, Ed.D.** is a dedicated pastor, leader, and educator with over 25 years of experience empowering both children and adults. She views her pastoral role as a profound privilege, serving the Lord by serving His people. As an educator, her passion lies in fostering meaningful learning experiences, whether in corporate, academic, or spiritual contexts. Dr. Green holds a doctorate from the University of Massachusetts Global, an MBA from the University of Phoenix, and a Master of Arts in Teaching from Brandman University, reflecting her commitment to lifelong learning and leadership.

**DINA HERNANDEZ, Ed.D.** is a dedicated leader and advocate in education, with over 25 years of service. Specializing in multilingual and multicultural education, Dr. Hernandez has consistently worked to champion equity and academic success. As an innovative leader, she has led initiatives to improve outcomes for historically marginalized and at-promise youth. Committed to equity, Dr. Hernandez has contributed significantly to designing and delivering professional development programs that support and empower educators and leaders.

**MARILOU RYDER, Ed.D.** is a university professor and women's leadership expert. With a decade leading large school districts, she understands firsthand the ever-changing landscape of women in the workplace. But she's more than an educator; she's a beacon of inspiration and empowerment. An author of twelve books, her Amazon bestsellers blend interviews and research to empower women to harness their personal power for confidence and influence. As the Program Chair for the doctoral program at UMass Global, she champions self-empowerment through evidence-based techniques, igniting others to face life's challenges with courage. Dr. Ryder's captivating speaking engagements, infused with humor, leave audiences inspired. Her accolades include Top Ten Businesswomen, California Administrator of the Year, and Orange County Professor of the Year, cementing her reputation as a dynamic leader in empowerment.

**TRICIA THOMPSON, Ed.D.** is a dedicated wife, mom, daughter, friend, and educator with a passion for empowering the often-unheard voices in education. With 24 years of experience in various educational roles, Dr. Thompson has consistently championed the needs of all students, ensuring they receive the support they deserve. Currently serving as an Assistant Superintendent for Student Support Services, she tirelessly leads initiatives designed to foster an inclusive and supportive learning environment for every student. Dr. Thompson has a passion for encouraging female leaders in the many roles she has had the opportunity to serve in. She wholeheartedly believes that female leadership is an essential component to a strong K-12 learning organization. Dr. Thompson's unwavering commitment to student advocacy and leadership makes her a true inspiration in the field of education.

## CAREER TRUTHS

*Respect lasts longer than approval.*

www.ingramcontent.com/pod-product-compliance
Lightning Source LLC
Chambersburg PA
CBHW071122090426
42736CB00012B/1986